FRANKLIN E. COURT

Pater and his Early Critics

ELS EDITIONS

© 1980 by Franklin E. Court

ELS Editions
Department of English
University of Victoria
Victoria, BC
Canada V8W 3W1
www.elseditions.com

Founding Editor: Samuel L. Macey

General Editor: Luke Carson

Printed by CreateSpace

English literary studies monograph series
ISSN 0829-7681 ; 21
ISBN-10 0-920604-40-4
ISBN-13 978-0-920604-40-3

CONTENTS

TO THE MEMORY OF
B. R. JERMAN

FOREWORD

This is a study of early critical evaluations of Walter Pater's writings. I have limited the choice of critics, first, to those who had some literary prominence at the time; and, second, to those who, in my estimation, best represent the spirit of the Victorian age as it continued to manifest itself in its criticism during the last thirty years of the nineteenth century. I have intentionally not carried the study to the critics, with the exception of Edmund Gosse, who were associated with the development of the "aesthetic movement." Omitted, therefore, are considerations of the reviews and critical articles, in particular, of Vernon Lee (Violet Paget), Lionel Johnson, George Moore, and Oscar Wilde. I have attempted, instead, to provide some impression of Pater's reputation during the years before he became inseparably linked with aestheticism. Gosse, though somewhat on the fringe of the movement, was, in his criticism, too much of a custodian of tradition to have been associated with any major new developments in modern critical theory.

There is good reason to believe that Pater was propelled into the twentieth century as the unwilling spokesman of the aesthetic movement. Time has shown that he had another, more important claim to literary importance and that was as the critic who shifted the art of criticism away from the ethical center affirmed by Ruskin, Arnold and others to a new sense of the importance of the work itself and the essentially relative nature of how it was to be judged by reader or spectator, irrespective of credentials. It was a fortunate accident of history that the aesthetic movement, for better or worse, should have kept his name before the public, for up to the 'nineties he had little solid support of any kind.

The problem of how Pater's reputation was faring in the early years of the twentieth century was recognized by George Saintsbury in 1906 in an article in *The Bookman*. It was twelve years after Pater's death and Saintsbury, a firm supporter, noted that signs were beginning to appear that indicated a healthy widening of interest in Pater and his works.[1] Not generally remembered for his unerring foresight, Saintsbury, nevertheless, pointed out a difficulty that he believed Pater critics would have to surmount—and that was, and still is, that Pater and Paterism were separate items.

The problem, he added, is made even more difficult in the light of mankind's remarkable tendency to take things "from the interpreters who occur" rather "than from the things themselves." Pater was easy to interpret, he noted, but difficult to understand. Understanding is partly a passive, inarticulate act; interpretation, by contrast, wholly articulate and wholly active. It is when the active process of interpretation is begun that people get into trouble and the dangers develop. Any critic, regardless of how objective he envisions himself, must exert a superhuman effort to keep from speaking and acting for himself; and, as Saintsbury suggested, "he will be clever indeed if he does not put that speech and that action in the place of his subject's" (p. 346). If a Cambridge interpreter produced a Pater portrait, he would produce a Cambridge Pater, more likely than not. Saintsbury believed that after a time, this particular danger would disappear. But before it did one would have to be on guard and to read Pater's critical interpreters very cautiously. One would have to be wary, in particular, of assuming that the criticism, even that done by the reputable and the prominent, provided an accurate assessment or interpretation of either Pater or Paterism. Nor should claims to personal knowledge be trusted. "I knew Mr. Pater myself," he admitted; "I had known him before the *Studies* [*Studies in the History of the Renaissance*] appeared, and I knew him after. But I do not think my personal knowledge of him helped me nearly so much to comprehend him and his work as the fact that, though I was a younger man by more than one Oxford generation, the days which we saw were, in a larger sense, the same days" (p. 347). How well Saintsbury himself comprehended Pater and his work, in spite of having shared "the same days," is questionable; but as a warning to students to be on the lookout for misreadings and misrepresentations, he was absolutely and unerringly on the mark.

In 1906, Saintsbury was warning primarily against critical interpretations of Paterism that had been published since the appearance of *The Renaissance* in 1873. Over the years that intervened, Pater's theories had been confused; the result, Saintsbury concluded, of unscrupulous satire, or "false brethren" who may have encouraged the satire further by their example, or "the natural inertia and gullibility of the public mind." It was comparatively unimportant if Pater had been simply misunderstood by the individual reader, but it was a very serious thing indeed if he had been misunderstood and if others should have followed that misunderstanding. The real irony of Saintsbury's concern, however, is that he did extremely little himself to provide an accurate assessment or interpretation of Pater or Paterism that would have served as an alternative to the misinterpretations. He was much too taken with the delicacies of Pater's prose to say anything substantial about him.

Much of this study deals with the lives, moral predilections, literary interests and credos, scientific biases, self-protective myths, and other relevant qualities of those figures who were instrumental in fashioning Pater's early reputation. It is based on the assumption that a critic's personal life is not separate from his works as long as his opinions either stress or imply a value judgment. Harold Bloom noted recently while discussing T. S. Eliot as critic, emphasizing in particular the impact that Eliot has had on Pater's reputation in the twentieth century: "Pater . . . is still out of fashion, having been dismissed by T. S. Eliot to the large limbo inhabited by those who did not keep literature in its proper relation to Christian belief."[2] How does one separate Eliot the Christian from Eliot the critic? In all fairness to Eliot perhaps it should not even be attempted. But in all fairness to Pater, for one, it should certainly be taken into consideration when Eliot's damning critical judgment is invoked. Looking back at the early criticisms of Pater and the lives, particularly, of the critics who made the judgments and subsequently created the myths, one discovers that, as Saintsbury warned, Pater was frequently misread and misrepresented; almost the sole exception, among the more prominent late-century commentators on his work, was John Morley; and then he seems not to have been given much serious consideration by later critics and interpreters. And so who was left to speak with authority for Pater and to assign him a fair and accurate position in the academic literary canon as it was conceived in the years shortly before and after the turn of the twentieth century?

9

CHAPTER I

Early Directions

The early years at Oxford were formative ones for Walter Pater. Those who knew him during those years were generally troubled by a certain lack of sincerity and a flippancy that, at times, verged on cynicism. He came up to Oxford as a student in 1858, graduated in 1862, and rented rooms on Oxford's High Street from which he tutored private pupils. In 1864, he was elected to a classical fellowship at Brasenose College and lived in a house with his sisters, Hester and Clara, until 1885, when he decided to divide his life between the academic quiet of Oxford and the more promising literary world of London. He and his sisters moved to London and there he spent his vacation periods, returning to Oxford during the academic terms.

In 1893, the year before his death, he left London for good and returned full time to the quiet, pleasant Oxford surroundings, to a life-style far more suited to his temperament. A. C. Benson, his first biographer, records that the Paters settled "in great contentment" in a house in St. Giles, "a quiet house with a plastered front of some antiquity, with a pleasant row of trees in front of it."[1] Benson quotes the carefully chosen words of T. H. Warren, one of Pater's colleagues, President of Magdalen College, on these later years: "Can I put it in a few words? He expressed life for himself and to others in terms of sensations, of impressions. These he might analyse, combine, and re-combine, but together they formed his working synthesis. I did not really know him in the earlier days, when in his written work the sensuousness and the referability of everything to sensation was so avowed. I only knew him well much later when he had become a kind of quietist: what the real man was I could not say."[2]

What the "real man" was, perhaps, will never be ascertained, owing to the scarcity of biographical materials. But the judgments and impressions of Pater left by his many critics and friends are available and can create for us, if not the man, then, at least, the impression that the man, viewed particularly through his works, left on those whose interest he captured.

Warren's reference to the avowed "sensuousness" and "referability of everything to sensation" that he associated with the early works rather accurately sums up the general critical opinion of Pater during the early years. And though the condemnation was largely undeserved, based often on inaccurate and prejudiced readings, it was so commonly believed that Pater's reputation as a man of letters never completely recovered.

Most of his adult life was centered on Oxford University; and, particularly in the early years, Oxford proved to be a chastising experience. During the years prior to 1873 when *Studies in the History of the Renaissance*, his first full length work, appeared, he had acquired a reputation as a bold critic of religion, especially Anglicanism, and as a philosopher of suspicious doctrines. That early impression was responsible for much of the hostility he encountered. On March 17, 1873, less than a month after the publication of *The Renaissance*, he received a letter from the Reverend John Wordsworth, an old friend who was at the time chaplain of Brasenose. Wordsworth's letter set the tone for Oxford's official reception of *The Renaissance*. Wordsworth registered his grief at the conclusions he believed Pater had arrived at in the book. "I owe so much to you in time past," he acknowledged, "and have so much to thank you for as a colleague more recently, that I am very much pained in making this avowal. But after a perusal of the book I cannot disguise from myself that the concluding pages adequately sum up the philosophy of the whole; and that that philosophy is an assertion, that no fixed principles either of religion or morality can be regarded as certain, that the only thing worth living for is momentary enjoyment and that probably or certainly the soul dissolves at death into elements which are destined never to reunite."[3] Wordsworth had overreacted and may have had the essays that Pater read before the Old Mortality Society in the 'sixties in mind, essays that supposedly averred Pater's disbelief in the immortality of the soul; for *The Renaissance* was hardly a direct attack on Christianity. And his subtle, self-disciplining and highly moralistic theory of the "moment" was equally misrepresented by Wordsworth. But given the reputation Pater had acquired at Oxford by this time, the appearance of the book with its defense of a theory of relativism and "art for art's sake" and its implied criticism of those, like Ruskin, who would judge art primarily by moral standards, it is little wonder that clerical Oxford decided to take it all very personally and, consequently, raised its ministerial guard.[4] Wordsworth noted, rather hypocritically in fact, in his letter that all would have been forgiven or, at least, overlooked if only Pater had remained anonymous. But to publish such heresy under his name as a Fellow of Brasenose was unforgivable: "Could you have known the grief your words would be to many of your Oxford contemporaries," he admonished, "you might even have found no ignoble pleasure in refraining from uttering them." He fervently appealed to Pater to relinquish his role as examiner in the divinity examination that at the time was a prerequisite for the bachelor's degree.[5]

If this kind of censure came from an old friend, what could he expect from those who felt no past debt? Indeed, condemnation of *The Rennaissance* at Oxford during Pater's early career seems not to have relaxed. In 1875, John Fielder Mackarness, Bishop of Oxford, in *A Charge Delivered to the Clergy of the Diocese of Oxford* chose to rail against the book, claiming "that to young men who have imbibed this teaching the Cross is an offence, and the notion of a vocation to teach it an unintelligible craze."[6] And Logan Pearsall Smith, in his reminiscences of Oxford at the end of the nineteenth century, recalls that even into the late 1880's Pater was still held at no account in Oxford, especially at Balliol College where "to maintain an ecstacy ... was by no means the Balliol conception of triumphant achievement." Smith recounts how Edmund Gosse once told him that when the memorial to Shelley was dedicated at University College in 1892 and famous British intellectuals and authors of the day were invited to attend, Pater was denied an invitation. Gosse himself had luncheon with Pater that day, expecting to accompany him to the unveiling. But Pater could not go, and a perplexed and disappointed Gosse was forced to go alone.[7]

The motives behind much of the negative early criticism of *The Renaissance* are suspect. Both at Oxford and in the published critical reviews, the tendency seems to have been over-reaction based either on an obtuse misreading of Pater's intention, as in the case of John Wordsworth, or on the inability to provide a judgment of the work untainted by personal crotchets or *ad hominem* diatribes that in large measure helped to fix Pater's reputation for years afterward as that of a spasmodic academic dilettante writing florid, outrageously ornamental prose—the kind of figure the reviewer for the *Saturday Review* had in mind when he took after the book for its "flights of imagination," its "heated rapture," and its "sickly" examples of "sugary writing." Even more damaging to Pater, however,

13

were his claims that Pater deified passion and then dared to offer Victor Hugo as a literary exemplar of his creed. Choosing Hugo as an example, he added, "says little for the soundness or sobriety of the system."[8] And so, from the outset, Pater was presented to the Victorian reading public as a gilt-edged pagan scribbler, seeking literary models in suspicious foreign ports. The picture did little to encourage a serious reception to his works —especially among strident Victorian Francophobes, and there were many, who felt only scrofulous winds blowing across the channel.

In spite of some scattered favorable commentary from critics like Edmund Gosse and John Morley, Pater's early reputation was affected most by his detractors. And one of the severest of these early opponents was Mrs. Margaret Oliphant, the renowned and widely popular Victorian novelist.

It is inadequate to assume that Mrs. Oliphant (1828-1897) censured *The Renaissance* simply because it offended her Victorian sense of moral propriety. The reason lies much deeper in her character. Like the reviewer from the *Saturday Review*, she based much of her judgment on simple personal prejudice. But her approach to the subject was in keeping with what she insisted a critic should do. Writing earlier, in 1871, in a review for *Blackwood's Edinburgh Magazine*, the periodical that published most of her reviews as well as a large portion of her fiction, she noted that "the true critic should see more than the book before him—he should see the mind that produced it."[9]

Regrettably, her review of *The Renaissance*, appearing in November 1873, was consistent with this theory; for in it, she argued away from the substance of the book and to the man or to the mind of the man she believed produced the book. She called *The Renaissance* "pretentious," a specimen "of a class removed from ordinary mankind by that ultra-culture and aca- demical contemplation of the world as a place chiefly occupied by other beings equally cultured and refined, which . . . forms an inner circle of Illuminati in almost every university"; this is a class "very different from those poor but daring adventurers of literature" she seems to have sup- ported, those who "cultivated the Muses on a little oatmeal." Her review was an attack directed primarily at the loftiness of Pater's academic and refined intentions—as she interpreted them. Specifically, she was bothered by claims for "self-culture," a pursuit that treats "all the great art and artists of the past, and all the centuries of men, as chiefly important and attractive in their relations to that Me who is the centre of the *dilettante's* world." She was a shrewd critic with a keen sensitivity for the feelings of her audience. Her works, and there were many—novels, biographies, histories, travel sketches, as well as criticism, were consistently written to appeal to a predominantly Church of England reading public, and she liked to poke fun at dissenting sects. At one point in the review of *The Renaissance* she associated Pater's artistic vision with low-church egotism. And though one strains to see any evident association between Pater's aesthetics and low-churchism, the effect such a claim must have had on an audience already suspicious of dissenters is noteworthy. The review concludes with an attack on a quality she calls "Greekness," and she ponders facetiously on the effect "Greekness" will have on Oxford's "Poor, young, too rich, too clever, too dull, too refined souls." She was evidently not at all in awe of the venerable institution. Visions like Pater's, she adds, conceived in limited, thin atmospheres like that, betray "the decay among us of all true and living art"—her final word on *The Renaissance*.[10]

From the outset, her criticism of the book takes issue more with how and under what circumstances it was written than it does with the substance of Pater's thought. The argument is carried not only to the man but also to the atmosphere that she believes establishes the tone of the man's life-style, the man's mind, an atmosphere that she associates with "ultra-culture," an "inner circle of Illuminati," dillettantism, "High Intellectualism," and "low-churchism," a world that she also insisted on linking with Oxford, a haven for the "too rich," the "too refined."

Why she went after Pater and the world she believed he reflected with such zeal is in keeping with her critical dicta but is even more understandable in the light of certain key circumstances that affected her own life and career. For Mrs. Oliphant herself was in many ways one of the "daring adventurers" she alludes to in the review, and like them she too frequently found herself in situations where she was forced to cultivate the muses on a little oatmeal. A look at her autobiography, published in 1899, two years after her death, reveals facets of her life that make her disdain for Pater and what she believed he represented much clearer.

The underlying tone of the autobiography is subdued resentment frequently verging on an acute sense of self pity. Writing in 1885, at the age of fifty-seven, even before the tragic early nineties during which she would lose her two remaining children—her beloved sons, Cyril and

Cecco—she acknowledges feeling extremely weary with her life and all of the work it had demanded: "I have not been able to rest, to please myself, to take the pleasures that have come in my way, but have always been forced to go on without a pause."[11] And, indeed, she was burdened all of her adult life with responsibilities—her own and others—that she insisted on assuming; her own pleasures seem to have been regularly subjected to the needs of those around her. In many ways, she was a very giving woman. She knew great suffering, poverty, and disillusionment, all of which contributed to an attitude of hard-headed common sense that colored her estimate of those who advocated or lived lives that she interpreted as being overly refined or free of similar sobering responsibilities.

Early in her life, she sadly watched her brother Willie's dissipation. After a brief experience as minister of a small Presbyterian church in a Northumberland village, at which he was a dismal failure, Willie returned to the family home where he settled down in idleness, smoked, read old novels and newspapers and, as she accounts, "most horrible of all, got to content himself with that life!" He remained financially dependent on her to the end of his life. She lost her young husband, Frank, in 1859. They were living in Italy at the time, and she was supporting the family with her writing and with the benevolent generosity of Blackwood's, Frank being much too ill to work. They had gone to Italy for his health. When he died, she became the sole provider. Later, after her return to England, she found herself in the tragic position of trying to salvage her brother Frank's marriage and, later, his life. When Frank could no longer support his family properly, she assumed responsibility for his children, raising his son and namesake, Frank Wilson, as though he were her own.

She now had three boys to educate: her own sons and young Frank Wilson, her nephew. She notes in the *Autobiography*:

It had to be done, and that was enough, and there is no doubt that it was much more congenial to me to drive on and keep everything going, with a certain scorn of the increased work [i.e., her writing], and metaphorical toss of my head, as if it mattered! than it ever would have been to labour with an artist's fervour and concentration to produce a masterpiece. One can't be two things or serve two masters. Which was God and which was mammon in that individual case it would be hard to say, perhaps; for once in a way mammon, meaning the money which fed my flock, was in a kind of a poor way God, so far as the necessities of that crisis went.[12]

She admittedly resented writers who did not have the responsibilities she had, and she envied their success. Her comments on George Eliot are particularly revealing. She observes: "How I have been handicapped in life! Should I have done better if I had been kept, like her, in a mental greenhouse and taken care of? . . . it is a little hard sometimes not to feel with Browning's Andrea that the men who have no wives, who have given themselves up to their art, have had an almost unfair advantage over us who have been given perhaps more than one Lucrezia to take care of." Clearly, she envisioned herself as an artist with an artist's desire for an honest commitment to the craft, but she believed that the responsibilities and demands made on her by her dependents forced her to sacrifice claims to artistic immortality for the price of the day's ration of oatmeal. An ironic self-deprecating humility develops out of this self-pity. Again speaking of George Eliot, she observes that "no one will mention me in the same breath," but she adds "that is just. It is a little justification to myself to think how much better off she was,—no troubles in all her life as far as appears. . . . And though her marriage is not one that most of us would have ventured on, still it seems to have secured her a worshipper unrivalled."[13] She must have resented George Eliot's literary connection with Lewes as well as her freedom to work at will—freedom she obviously believed that she did not have. Her final, curious judgment on Eliot is more self-revealing than critical: George Eliot "must have been a dull woman with a great genius distinct from herself."[14]

Her envy of more successful writers whose lives were easier is directly in line with her attacks in the review of *The Renaissance* on "ultra Culture," on authors she associated particularly with the university. Ironically, in later years, a large share of her self-sacrificing hard work would go to insure an Oxford education for her two sons. But the extent of her disdain for intellectualism in the ivory tower was extreme. In an 1879 letter to Blackwood, sent while she was living in Oxford, she warned that "intellectualism, like every other *ism*, is monotonous, and the timidity and mutual alarm of the younger potentates strikes me a good deal. . . . Scholarship is a sort of poison tree, and kills everything."[15] Earlier, in another letter to Blackwood, written in response to a negative comment on her reviewing, dated 6 February 1873 (the same year Pater's *Renaissance* appeared), she informed Blackwood, "I can only review books at all on the condition that I express my own feelings in respect to them. . . .

The tremendous applause which has greeted this performance is a good specimen of the sort of thing I am anxious to struggle against—the fictitious reputation got up by men who happen to be 'remembered at the Universities,' and who have many connections among literary men."[16] But her scorn for literary men, intellectualism, and the easy life-styles she associated with universities came back to haunt her in later years: in 1894, she pondered that possibly her son Cyril, who was never a serious student, did poorly at Oxford and never settled successfully into any career (he died in 1890) after his Oxford years because she had created a climate of scorn for such things, a climate that made it difficult for him to take academic pursuits seriously. Now, in 1894, in her old age, lonely and grief-stricken, she sorrowfully acknowledges having had a "foolish way of laughing at the superior people, the people who took themselves too seriously—the boys of pretension, and all the strong intellectualisms. This gave him [Cyril], perhaps, or helped to form, a prejudice against the good and reading men, who have so many affectations . . . and led him towards those so often inferior, all inferior to himself, who had the naturalness along with the folly of youth."[17]

Mrs. Oliphant was a hard-headed, resilient, and industrious critic; but the majority of her judgments, rather than being informative were simply shrewd. Her most recent biographers suggest that her problem was an inability to see beyond the "personal estimate"; she tenaciously looked to her own life and personal struggles and responded impatiently to views that differed too much from hers. This lack of critical detachment produced in her criticism a blind affinity only for what was in her estimation the healthy-minded and wholesome; she was repelled by extremes of any kind; she insisted that a writer should write for the average, for common people of ordinary understanding and simple virtue. Highest value was placed on moderation, a characteristic that helps to explain why, for instance, she found Heathcliff in *Wuthering Heights* unappealing and why she thought Hardy's *Tess of the d'Urbervilles* sordid.[18] Willie Tulloch, on "Mrs. Oliphant" for *The Bookman* in August 1897, the year of her death, said of her later years: "somehow it seemed to me she could never quite understand and sympathize with those who took views differing from her own, and she was not slow to pour ridicule on you and your favorites if they were not hers."[19]

It is reasonable to explain Mrs. Oliphant's hostility to Pater by saying that it expresses a consistent, unconscious need to strike out at privilege and unconventionality. In Pater she believed that she had encountered both. But whether we excuse her or not, given the difficulties of her unselfish struggle to produce a livelihood, the fact remains that Pater's reputation suffered at her hands. She judged *The Renaissance* mainly on the basis of the atmosphere she thought had produced it, a judgment that clearly reflects her disdain for a level of intellectualism and refinement that she associated with universities and university men, and a fear of unwholesome extremes she thought Pater's philosophy capable of creating. By appealing to public prejudice, no less than the reviewer from the *Saturday Review*, she assisted in the creation of an attitude of suspicion that colored the work's reception and that continued to mar Pater's standing as a critic of the arts and aesthetic theory. George Eliot, shortly after reading Mrs. Oliphant's review, wrote to John Blackwood, "I agreed very warmly with the remarks made by your contributor this month on Mr. Pater's book, which seems to me quite poisonous in its false principles of criticism and false conceptions of life."[20] One wonders how warmly she would have responded to the reviewer's remarks if she had known what the reviewer thought of her. But Mrs. Oliphant's review was now public property and it could be waved like a banner by those who took exception to the theories of criticism and aesthetics that Pater advocated. Indeed, as late as 1883, ten years after Mrs. Oliphant's review, Henry James Nicoll noted, echoing Mrs. Oliphant's earlier language, that Pater's essays had been assailed because of "the supreme position they assign to art, and as being permeated by the tone of *an inner circle of illuminati*" (italics mine).[21] The irony is that Mrs. Oliphant's judgment actually said little that dealt specifically with either Pater's theory of criticism or his theory of aesthetics.

Her criticism of Pater did not end with the 1873 review of *The Renaissance*. In 1890, while reviewing *Appreciations: With An Essay on Style*, she, not surprisingly, criticized his stylistic quirks; but the most damaging criticism she reserved, once again, for her conception of him as the avatar of a world of academic refinement. When not referring to him by name, she calls him "our Professor," "our learned instructor," "elegant Don." He represented, she claims, "a very high example of the development theory," brought into being by "a slowly growing climax of intellectual over-production, and the artificiality of art." And his life "under the

19

sheltering walls of an old college, where the chief thing to be arrived at is a mild and refined superiority to your fellows" is contrasted with the life of Grant Allen, who was in her eyes a far more agreeable writer because he lived, by contrast, "outside in the fierce swirls and eddies of an ocean where every strong swimmer must keep his head above water as he can, and . . . makes no assertion of abstract superiority."[22] One gets the distinct impression looking at Mrs. Oliphant's reviews and her notion of life as an endurance run that she was dissatisfied with both her life and her career. Her critical judgments carry less weight now, but at the time she was a popular and influential literary figure, and the effect she had on the shaping of Pater's reputation was considerable.

Oxford was, for Pater, in many ways, a two-edged sword. He was attacked by many of his colleagues for not living up to the rigid clerical ideals of the institution, and by those outside, like Mrs. Oliphant, for the "abstract superiority," "ultra-culture," and "High Intellectualism" that she associated with university life.

Another critic who assailed him during those early years, but whose condemnation had a more far reaching effect eventually than Mrs. Oliphant's, was W. H. Mallock (1849-1923), satirist, student of social and economic theory, and a vocal critic of socialism. Mallock did much to distort Pater's image in the popular imagination, presenting him as a semi-conscious, rhapsodic dilletante. In *The New Republic*, a work serialized originally in 1876 in *Belgravia: An Illustrated London Magazine*, he created Mr. Rose, a satirical caricature of Pater. Rose is identified offhandedly for the guests assembled for the weekend at Otho Laurence's villa as a "pre-Raphaelite" who "always speaks in an undertone," and whose two topics are "self-indulgence and art."[23] The first installment of the serial appeared in June; by the time the final installment appeared in December, the work had attracted enough popular attention to convince the firm of Chatto and Windus to publish it in 1877 in two volumes. The work's authorship during this time, however, remained anonymous. Finally, in 1878, a new one volume edition appeared with Mallock's name boldly on the title page.

Mallock openly and frequently acknowledged throughout his life his support for principles he associated with tory idealism and High Anglicanism. He was an arch-conservative, insisting on the preservation of order and the *status quo*, particularly in religious matters and in matters related to the distribution of wealth. He was, also, a staunch and outspoken opponent of all forms of radicalism, or what he referred to in his *Memoirs* as " 'advanced' thought," and which he believed primarily responsible for the "mischief, religious, social, and political" that plagued the times. He began work on *The New Republic* during his second year of residence as an undergraduate at Oxford, his satirical talent fired by an immediate, intense dislike of the political and religious liberalism that he associated with the Oxford world.[24]

His dislike for "advanced thought" alone could account to a large extent for his humorously barbed satire on Pater's aestheticism. But he also took the liberty of toying freely with his personality. The most damaging allegation he makes in *The New Republic* links Pater's aestheticism directly with homosexuality. At one point, the dreamy Mr. Rose, who appears in the early books half-asleep or drugged most of the time, claims that he rather looks "upon life as a chamber, which we decorate as we would decorate the chamber of the woman or the youth that we love." Rose also slyly ingratiates himself with Lady Grace by helping her page, "a pretty boy with light curling hair, to arrange some tumblers on the grass."[25] When he is not being deceptively lascivious, he works himself into silly raptures on the subject of exquisite living and the high thrills of moments. Or when not hinting at vague homosexual yearnings or languidly murmuring to himself about the joys of the aesthetic life, Rose indulges in statements that are simply absurd; at one point, he recalls a "delicious walk" that he took along the Thames hoping to see "some unfortunate cast herself from the Bridge of Sighs."[26] But by far, the greater part of what Rose contributes to the weekend discussions, especially in the later books when he seems to rise from his stupor, involves a particular attitude toward history and culture, an attitude that Mallock directly associated with Rose's self-indulgent aestheticism.

Mallock was a serious student of history and economics. His interest in the historical process and the lessons for the present that it taught is reflected in his works on economics and social theory. Part of his lifetime argument with liberalism and particularly socialism involved his insistence on the need to make the past relevant and useful in the present, to produce a vision of an ordered historical continuum. Writing, for instance, in the strongly anti-socialistic *Aristocracy and Evolution,* a work he published in 1898, he argues that every human being is an inheritor of the past but

21

that men tend to inherit the past in varying degrees—"they inherit the knowledge of the past only according to the degree to which they acquire it; the language of the past only according to their skill in manipulating it; the inventions of the past only according to their skill in reproducing and using them."[27] Evident here and elsewhere in Mallock's studies is a concept of history viewed as an organism that must be seen whole and continual. To treat past ages or events in a vaccum without tying them to the present is to be guilty of what he calls—in *Property and Progress*, published in 1884—"stationary barbarism." It was the *lacuna*, the fundamental error in thought that he insisted formed the basis of socialistic theory. "For the process of civilization is a double one," he argues. "It consists, not only in satisfying wants that are inevitably felt, but in building up a fabric of new wants."[28] The past is man's inheritance, a valued investment for the present. Particularly important to Mallock was history viewed in terms of man's religious inheritance. In his *Memoirs* he writes of the need to test consistently the credibility of religion, meaning Christianity, "in the indirect effects produced by it on the quality of life generally."[29] In other words, if the quality of life has improved or deteriorated over the past nineteen hundred years, then it is largely due to the corresponding increase or decrease in religious credibility. In the nineteenth century, with religious orthodoxy seriously threatened by "advanced" philosophical and scientific theories, the quality of life must correspondingly deteriorate unless "a rational development of conservative thought" rescues the age and the true faiths—"on which the sanctities, the stabilities, and the civilization of the social order depend"—be revived. For without religion, he concludes, "life is reduced to absurdity."[30]

It is in the light of such thoughts on history and the place of religion in it that Mallock's attack on Pater as Mr. Rose should be understood. For he devotes much more time to exposing and satirizing Rose's aesthetic attitude toward the past than he does to Rose's insipid homosexuality.

The first mention of Rose's imagination being significantly fired by anything comes in Book III when the group's discussion of history seems finally to arouse him from semi-consciousness. "Why, but for history," he exclaims:

what should we be now but a flock of listless barbarians . . . ? Would not all life's choicer and subtler pleasures be lost to us, if Athens did not still live to redeem us from the bondage of the middle age, and if the Italian Renaissance—that strange child of Aphrodite and Tann-haüser, did not still live to stimulate us out of the torpor of the present age? What, but for history, should we know ... of the χáρις of Greece, of the lust of Rome, of the strange secrets of the Borgias? Consider, too, the bowers of quiet, full of sweet dreams, that history will always keep for us—how it surrounds the house of the present with the boundless gardens of the past—gardens rich in woods, and waters, and flowers, and outlooks on illimitable seas. Think of the immortal dramas which history sets before us; of the keener and profounder passions which it shows in action, of the exquisite groups and figures it reveals to us, of nobler mould than ours—Harmodius and Aristogeiton, Achilles and Patroclus, David and Jonathan, our English Edward and the fair Piers Gaveston ..., or, above all, those two by the agnus castus and the plane-tree where Ilyssus flowed ... and where the Attic grasshoppers chirped in shrill summer choir.[31]

In this passage, Mr. Rose nimbly divests history of most of its inherited value, making it ineffectual as the active means through which man might improve the quality of the present age. Instead of recognizing the need to inherit and use the past, as Mallock urged, Rose holds up the promise of history as a static but aesthetic means of escape from "the torpor of the present age." History becomes a fanciful dream vision surrounding "the house of the present with ... boundless gardens." This is history gutted and boned—Mallock's "stationary barbarism"; the great lessons and events of the past, including the great moral teachings of Christianity, have no more significance to Rose than the imagined chirps of so many Attic grass-hoppers.

His discussion of the meaning of history concluded, Rose moves on in an attempt to explain the link between his thoughts on history and the subject of culture, one that, not surprisingly, particularly interests Mr. Luke (Matthew Arnold). The aim of culture, Rose suggests, is to "make the soul a musical instrument." The man of culture, when only a mere passive observer of life, is like "an Aeolian harp, which the winds at will play through."[32] Passivity then is the key for Rose to acquiring culture; for the man of culture envisions himself as a passive observer of history rather than as an active participant. In response to Mr. Herbert's question (Herbert is Ruskin) "How would your culture alter and better the present, if its powers were equal to its wishes?" Rose responds by citing his walks around London and the hideousness of what he sees in the present: "the shapeless houses, the forest of ghastly chimney-pots, . . . the hell of distracting noises. . . . " The only thing that saves him from despair, he notes, are the shops of certain upholsterers and dealers in works of art. For there in the perfect pattern of some fabric or on a design for wallpaper or some old china vase, Rose finds happiness and true beauty. And he advises Mr. Herbert, in a particularly pointed passage, that "there is amongst us a growing number who have deliberately turned their backs on all these things, and have thrown their whole souls and sympathies into the happier art-ages of the past. They have gone back. . . . To such men the clamour, the interests, the struggles of our own times, become as meaningless as they really are. . . . several distinguished artists . . . will, on principle, never admit a newspaper into their houses that is of later date than the times of Addison; and I have good trust that the number of such men is on the increase—men . . . who with a steady and set purpose follow art for the sake of art, beauty for the sake of beauty, love for the sake of love, life for the sake of life."[33]

Mallock's satire could not be more clearly directed. Rose's aestheticism carries with it an implicit disregard for history, religion, and, in particular, the needs of the historical present. The present, in fact, is only valuable for what it preserves of the static, imaginary art-ages of the past as defense against the hideousness of the present. The argument is ingenious; and though Rose's theory of the significance of history is intended as a satire on what Mallock believed was Pater's theory of history, Mallock's interpretation is wrong.

To begin with, nowhere in *The Renaissance* does Pater even suggest either that the Renaissance or any other age should be studied in a vacuum or that the present is only valuable for what is preserved in it from the past. Actually, the Renaissance as an historical era extends for Pater from at least the thirteenth to the eighteenth centuries. His theory of history is linked far more closely with his theory of greatness. What is of utmost importance, he suggests, is not the measure of what has survived but is, instead, that the critic or historian investigating an age discover in whom "the genius, the sentiment of the period" is best reflected. "Who was the receptacle of its refinement, its elevation, its taste," he asks. And, quoting William Blake, he concludes, "The ages are all equal . . . but genius is always above its age."[34] Pater and Rose, in spite of the humorous appeal of the parody, actually have little in common. Rose's incessant ramblings in defense of passive aestheticism carry with them an implicit disregard for the historical present. But Pater, by contrast, clearly insists in the "Conclusion," for one example, on the need for regular, continuous testing of new opinions and for challenging the desire to acquiesce in facile orthodoxies of any kind—a warning that applied to past as well as to present orthodoxies.

Yet it was exactly that kind of challenge to orthodoxy, including the implicit challenge to conservative religious orthodoxy, and his defense of the relative nature of all knowledge, that Mallock associated with the kind of "advanced" thinking he found objectionable.

There is, however, another less obvious reason for Mallock's disenchantment with Pater's *Renaissance*. And that is its implicit criticism of Ruskin. Mallock was an acknowledged and vocal supporter of Ruskin. Recalling his Oxford years in his *Memoirs*, he writes of the loyalty he felt toward Ruskin at that time and of his sympathy with his genius. Ruskin, he notes, was "the only human being . . . who held and publicly expressed views similar to my own, so far as I knew."[35] He also acknowledges being forever haunted by Ruskin's voice, after listening to his lectures.[36] He put into the mouth of Mr. Herbert, his portrait of Ruskin in *The New Republic*, the few words that seem to ring true. As a knowledgeable disciple of Ruskin, Mallock could hardly have overlooked the anti-Ruskinian critical implications, particularly in Pater's "Preface."

In the "Preface" Pater responds directly to Ruskin's case against the Renaissance as an immoral age. He claims superiority for a "certain kind of temperament" that, unlike Ruskin's, can see beyond ages and milieus to the value of individual works of genius. The question the critic should ask, he argues, is not the question prompted by Ruskin's criticism, that is, how moral or immoral the age was; instead, he should discover in whom the genius of the period is reflected. Though Mallock, in his portrait of Rose, never directly counters Pater's implicit criticism of Ruskin—in fact, he never openly acknowledges it—nevertheless, it seems only reasonable that it would have colored his disenchantment with Pater's vision of history, compounding the already disagreeable feeling he had toward the immorality as well as the offensive historical and aesthetic position that he believed Pater advocated. Viewing Mallock's satirical treatment of Pater against this background makes more convincing Mallock's observation, in a letter to Thomas Wright, that the Rose portrait "was meant to represent an attitude of mind rather than a man."[37] But in spite of his disclaimer, Mallock never took any public position on the Rose portrait that would have alleviated even a portion of the damage that it had done to Pater's early reputation.[38]

The Mr. Rose portrait reportedly caused Pater a great deal of grief, so much so that some critics believe it was primarily responsible for his withdrawing the "Conclusion" from the second edition of *The Renaissance* in 1877. But Pater's reasons for withdrawing the "Conclusion" are uncertain. Edmund Gosse suggested that he withdrew the "Conclusion" because he was upset with the persistence with which the newspapers attributed to him all sorts of "aesthetic" extravagances; but Gosse also believed that Pater was flattered by the Mr. Rose portrait and that, because he was young and obscure, he decided that to be included among such distinguished company, even in ridicule, was a compliment.[39] If Mallock's attack had the impact on Pater's decision that some believe, then it is probably more reasonable to conclude that Pater would have recognized in Mallock's satire elements of his thought that involved much more than just the arguments raised in the "Conclusion." But the portrait did cause him grave concern.

The final irony, however, is that although most of Mallock's criticism of Mr. Rose is based on Rose's devitalizing conception of history and culture, it was not the vision of Mr. Rose on history and culture that caught the popular imagination after and subsequent to the publication of *The New Republic*; it was, instead, the vision of Mr. Rose the languishing, sexual deviate. Mallock's satirical portrait had a remarkably adverse effect on Pater's reputation—in spite of the select minority of writers it associated him with. Long after the turn of the century, some readers and students of the age would still be unable to distinguish that particular caricature from the man.

Mallock had not been the only critic to assail Pater for his treatment of history. Nor was he the only one to challenge specifically his interpretation of the Renaissance as history. As early as 1873, while reviewing *The Renaissance* for *Nation*, W. J. Stillman (1828-1901), a rather prominent late-century American art critic and landscape painter and, significantly, a longtime friend and early devotee of Ruskin, accused Pater of taking a logically inadmissable liberty with the term.[40] Clearly indebted to Ruskin, Stillman claimed that Pater mistakenly applied the term to a period in time marked by the decay of art. He argued that any art that looks back to classical times, as Renaissance art supposedly did, ceases to be art and, instead, becomes artifice. "A renaissance that is the renewal of dead forms," he adds, "is not a new birth, it is a galvanic resuscitation; and the modern sympathy . . . with the Renaissance so-called, is but a modern abhorrence of life and health, and fondness for death and artifice." At another point in the review, Stillman makes another observation, equally Ruskinian in spirit. He claims that in spite of certain peculiar developments in the national temperament, "there will be art" as long "as there is genuine and lofty emotion."[41] The implication is reminiscent of Ruskin's notion that ethics and epochs when considered together produce easily discernible formulas; in particular, with Stillman, the theory holds that no unexalted age can produce genuine and serious art. Pater's conception of the Renaissance was all wrong, therefore, because he wrongly associated the idea of rebirth with a period in time that Stillman insisted was distinctly characterized by decay. But ever present behind these claims is the shadow of Ruskin; no less clearly visible here than he would be later in Mallock's destructive portrait of Mr. Rose.

Stillman makes Pater out to be an ingenuous dilletante. He criticizes him not because of the theory of aesthetics or criticism that is the substance of the book or even, which is more likely, for his stylistic peculiarities (surprisingly he finds merit in its "charm of style" and in Pater's handling of poetry); but, instead, he takes issue with him as a misdirected art historian and because he promoted a theory of Renaissance that was contrary to that advocated by the formidable and, for the time, far more influential figure of Ruskin. One cannot fault Ruskin for the critical shortcomings of his disciples, but there is a certain disturbing lack of justice about the type of criticism found in Stillman's review as well as in Mallock's portrait of Mr. Rose. A fair and impartial review of Pater's work was impossible as long as critics insisted on such unbalanced and prejudicially comparative measures of judgment. In the case of Stillman and Mallock, in particular, Pater's reputation suffered, not for his controversial theory of aesthetics but primarily because his treatment of history was suspect. And it was suspect, mainly, because it was not Ruskin's.

Another disenchanted critic who challenged Pater's treatment of history, but whose disenchantment had little to do with Ruskin's influence, was Mrs. Mark Pattison (1840-1904).[42] Her 1873 review of *The Renais-*

sance was as myopic in its own way as Stillman's, though in all probability, because of her social position, it was more damaging. The wife of the famous rector of Oxford's Lincoln College, and after his death and her remarriage, known to the literary world as Lady Dilke, Mrs. Pattison eventually became a close acquaintance of Pater. After his death, she is reported to have bound the copy of *The Renaissance* that he had personally given to her more beautifully than any other book in her collection and to have placed his portrait reverently within it. Sir Charles Dilke— her second husband, who made this observation—suggests that it may well have been done in penance for her earlier review.[43]

Though her home until the death of Mark Pattison in 1884 was Oxford, she was determined not to be stifled by its solemnities. She was free spirited and "continental"; her working room at Oxford is said to have been filled with French engravings and books—mostly foreign—on travel and the fine arts. And, as an example of her free spirit, it is recorded that, on occasion, she even smoked in public. But she was in addition a knowledgeable and respected art critic, and it is hardly likely that she would have been put off by Pater's *Renaissance*, however unconventional its aestheticism may have seemed to clerical Oxford. But though not critical at all of his aesthetic theories, she still gave the book a most desultory and damaging review when it appeared in 1873.

Her first critical reaction to the book was directed at its title; she claimed that the title misled by suggesting that the work was a history of Renaissance art. The point is valid, of course, though certainly minor. But Pater, who liked her and had respect for her judgment, seems to have seriously attended to her objection by changing the title of the second edition in 1877, dropping the offending word, "History," so that the title read *The Renaissance: Studies in Art and Poetry* rather than the original *Studies in the History of the Renaissance*. He may have hoped to eliminate as well, by altering the title, any future possibilities of the book being again misread as a history, as Stillman had done in 1873 and Mallock in 1876, the year before the second edition appeared.

Mrs. Pattison's objection to the misleading nature of the earlier title is understandable, but what follows from that objection is misdirected and inconsistent with the obvious objectives of the book. All of which suggests that she simply may not have known what to make of it—and she had not been the only one. For though she admitted that it was not a history, acknowledging at the outset of her review that "the historical element is precisely that which is wanting," she followed up this acknowledgement by condemning the book because it was not a contribution to the *historical* study of Renaissance art and culture.[44] Now this is like assuming that, owing to its title, Samuel Butler's *The Way of All Flesh* is an erotic book or Ruskin's *Sesame and Lilies* is a horticultural study, and then condemning them because they fail to measure up. The logic is perverse. A more open-minded reading of *The Renaissance* should have revealed, without delving too far into the text, that Pater's observations on Renaissance art and history, regardless of the title, were not intended to be read as prescriptive conclusions based on scientific, authoritative historical investigation. But if the book was not an art history, as the title suggested, then what was it? The problem was vexing; where was the precedent for work like Pater's—vignettes, portraits, that could hardly stand on their merits as biography and yet provided no intelligible or consistent way of looking at Renaissance art or history?

Mrs. Pattison seems to have solved the problem by assuming that since the book purported to be an art history, it was as an art history that she would review it. Consequently, she brought to bear on the book, her strong interest in history and, in particular, her rigid preoccupation at the time with the demanding analytical techniques of scientific historical research. She accused Pater, for instance, of not using the "scientific method," preferring instead to detach his subject from the historical setting and "to suspend it isolated . . . as if it were . . . a kind of air-plant independent of the ordinary sources of nourishment." And although she found merit in his "brilliantly accurate" choice of words, she warned that brilliant words "are not history, nor are they even to be relied on for accurate statement of simple matters of fact."[45]

Her review, in all respects, was consistent with her fixed conception of what she insisted research into periods of art history should entail. She was an acknowledged authority on French Renaissance art and culture. In 1879 she published a two-volume work on *The Renaissance of Art in France*, a carefully detailed, historically researched study of French Renaissance art, divided very methodically into separate sections on architecture, sculpture, painting, enamelling, and pottery. As a reference text for specialists it had some value; but it could hardly have had much appeal for the general reader. Nevertheless, Pater was impressed—particularly with her treatment of French architecture, a subject that interested him as well. And he also counted her among his friends. Earlier—in 1877, in a letter to Edmund Gosse—he commended an article that she had published on French architecture in *Contemporary Review*, an article later incorporated into chapter two of the first volume of her book.[46] She was a scrupulous scholar—and ironically that was probably why she did not give Pater a fair reading. Her early work is characterized by a pedantic severity that even Sir Charles W. Dilke, her second husband, was forced to admit, but he added in her defense that it was primarily the result of the dominant influence on her work of her husband, Mark Pattison.

Dilke had in mind a particularly smothering pedantic insistence on rigorous research methodology at the expense, oftentimes, of the readability of the text or, worse, the expense of any simple joy in the task. It was just such an insistence that must have prompted her as a young writer in 1868, while reviewing an art book for *Saturday Review*, to make the disheartening observation that " 'an author cannot be lively and amusing' when treating of the object of his life's labours."[47] Mrs. Humphry Ward, while recalling her Oxford years and the relationship between the Pattisons, remembered that when she had known Mrs. Pattison, she was already a scholar, adding the significant qualification—"even as her husband counted scholarship!"[48] Mark Pattison most clearly exemplified "deliberate impotence" to John Morley, who reviewed his memoirs when they were published in 1885. Morley writes that Pattison himself acknowledged as his life's motto the depressing expression, "Quicquid his operis fiat poenitet" ["Whatever work this one may do he is displeased with"]. Supposedly, scholarship for Pattison was characterized by a dreary emphasis on rigorous scientific labor; his obsession was with technique, methodology, especially one that carried the emphasis on detail and thoroughness to a deadening extreme. For Pattison, it produced laudable and flawless results; but, if Morley is correct, the price demanded for such precision was devitalizing. In terms of the response to Pater's *Renaissance*, the irony is that Pattison actually should have found much to admire and support. Pattison, in his own work on eighteenth-century deism, had attempted a serious investigation into the relative quality of the development of religious opinion without recourse to fixed formulas. And it was Pattison, as Morley observed, who was among the earliest to advocate the idea that what is most important to know about any age are the complex elements of moral feeling and character out of which opinions grow; and that knowledge requires an understanding of the *relative* nature of the advancement of opinion, religious or otherwise, without recourse to absolutes or dogmatic formulas. If what Dilke and Mrs. Ward suggest about Mrs. Pattison's deference to her husband on matters of scholarship is true, then one would expect both of the Pattisons to have been in complete sympathy with Pater's defense of the doctrine of relativity in *The Renaissance*, but there is no recognition in Mrs. Pattison's review of that aspect of the book. Instead, Pater is taken to task for his improper methodology.[49]

Mrs. Pattison was younger than her first husband by almost thirty years. They had been married in 1861 when she was twenty-one. In 1863, she notes, her husband suggested that if she wished to command respect, she must make herself "*the* authority on some one subject."[50] Her subject became Renaissance French art. The respect and admiration she retained throughout his lifetime for Mark Pattison as a scholar is expressed in her account of the long period before his death during which she nursed him: "if one life is to give way to the other, I feel sure it should be mine; his is worth much more—it represents much more, of much greater value to the world than mine. I think he is the only truly learned man I know."[51] They had been married twenty-three years. Pattison died in 1884; fourteen months after his death, she married Sir Charles Dilke.

Mrs. Pattison's review of *The Renaissance* was based on an unfortunate misinterpretation of Pater's motives. It is impossible to prove that Mark Pattison was responsible for the misdirected judgment; it was her review. And Pattison and Pater were supposedly close friends, often discussing books together.[52] But, regardless of where the source of the severity was located, the damage was done. Again, Pater had been the victim of an obtuseness—but this time, an obtuseness associated less with a complex of moral or personal predilections or critical fealties than with a simple excess of pedantic zeal. It is well to remember when recalling the position Mrs. Pattison had in the early formation of Pater's literary image, that the book she found so much fault with in 1873 was also the book that, as Sir Charles Dilke remembered, twenty years later, after Pater's death, she had bound more beautifully than any other in her collection. In 1887, three years after Pattison's death, she reviewed Pater's *Imaginary Portraits*. Fourteen years had elapsed since the appearance of the review of *The*

Renaissance. The change in tone is distinct and noteworthy; the review is highly commendatory. In the review of *The Renaissance* she faulted him for his factual inaccuracies and criticized him for studying individuals in isolation without sufficient reference to the historical context in which they lived. This time, though the work was not history, and there could be no confusion, nevertheless, she intentionally singled out for praise the presence of Pater himself in the portraits—an evanescence that she claims is how Pater sees himself reflected "in the mirror of past days" and that she also found in *Marius the Epicurean.* She also praises the portraits for being reflections of "some of the most interesting currents" affecting the thought of the times.[53] Ironically, the virtues she cites as the strengths of *Imaginary Portraits* were, had she been able to see them at the time, strengths that characterized *The Renaissance.*

The change in tone may be accounted for by a change in her position on the relative nature of critical assessments coupled with a growing appreciation over the years for Pater's aesthetics. Dilke recalls that by 1883 she had developed a genuine appreciation for the relative nature of aesthetic judgments, and he notes that this appreciation had become her "chief art doctrine." It was explained in 1883, he claims, in her account of the Burlington House Exhibition published in *Academy,* in which she argued that "aesthetic perceptions adjust themselves with sensitive instinct to find the means of translating the new moral aspect of things into corresponding aspects of colour and of form." And she added, "however incomplete and offensive the works of the modern innovators of today may seem to us . . . , however poor or absurd their methods of work may appear, we cannot ignore the fact that it is possibly to them that the future belongs."[54] But Mrs. Pattison's praise in 1887 was too little, too late. Earlier reviews of *The Renaissance,* including her own, had created an image of Pater as an historian of art and culture—and a rather bad one at that—that lasted through the 'seventies and well into the 'eighties. Even with the appearance of *Marius* in 1885, Pater still had a difficult time convincing those who insisted on measuring the value of the novel in terms of how accurately it portrayed life in second-century Rome that he was writing as a novelist and not as an historian.[55]

John Addington Symonds (1840-1893), poet, historian, critic of literature and the fine arts, at least, attempted to deal with Pater as a critic rather than an art historian; though implicit in most of what he wrote or said about Pater that has survived is the contention that as a critic of the arts, Pater not only had little of value to offer but his aestheticism as well was suspect and socially damaging.

Symonds also reviewed *The Renaissance* in 1873. And though, ironically, later critics, especially after Pater's subsequent positive review of the first volume of Symonds' *Renaissance in Italy* in 1875, insisted on linking them as kindred souls (Max Beerbohm, for one, observed that if fate had thrown Pater out of Oxford, he would have become merely another John Addington Symonds), the unavoidable truth is that Symonds envisioned himself rather as Pater's antagonist. In a letter written in February of 1873, a month before his review of *The Renaissance* appeared, he avowed that Pater's view of life gave him the "creeps"; adding as well that Pater's effort to explain it "to the world has in it a wormy-hollow-voiced seductiveness of a fiend."[56] On the surface, the review was sugar-coated, in order not to offend Pater; but a closer look reveals that he believed that Pater's aestheticism produced critical voluptuaries unable to discriminate the first rate from the worthless. He claimed that Pater was fascinated with decay and corruption and his critical method was "isolated, indifferent to common tastes and sympathies." He associated him with intellectual sybarites "careless of maintaining at any cost a vital connection with the universal instincts of humanity." His conclusion: Pater's aesthetic temperament was deficient and even caused him "to make mistakes of criticism," especially in his judgment of Botticelli as being ambivalent toward Catholicism.[57]

But sentiments that Symonds may have hoped to conceal in the 1873 review of *The Renaissance* were more openly revealed later in an essay entitled "Is Music the Type or Measure of All Art?" that he published in 1890 in *Essays Speculative and Suggestive*. Though he acknowledged being in agreement with Pater on a number of critical points, he accused him of exceeding the limits of good sense when he made the claim that all arts aspire in common to the condition of music. He also found highly questionable Pater's subsequent notion that the fine arts, because they aspire to a musical condition, must accordingly aspire toward a concurrent vagueness of intellectual intention; that is, the notion, he concluded, "that the delight of the eye or of the ear is of more moment than the thought of the brain"; or, quoting Pater on the subject, art strives always "to be independent of the mere intelligence." Ingenious though the idea may be, he asserted, if carried to its logical extreme, we might then have to prefer classic Japanese screen painting to the obviously superior Raphael's "School of Athens."[58]

Assuredly, if Symonds were alive these days, he would have to admit that for a substantial number of art specialists, Japanese screen painting does have a decided preference. But Symonds was confident of the tenability of his judgment. The time was 1890, and his world, in spite of its sophisticated and genteel veneer, was insulated, tightly European, and protectively Western. Ingenuous as his remark now appears to us, it nevertheless points up a very revealing and important difference between his and Pater's position in the history of art criticism; and it also is a clear indicator of why Symonds was unable to attribute any serious value to Pater's brand of art criticism; quite simply, Pater, whose interests he insisted were indifferent to "common tastes," was not democratic enough for him.

Symonds was a student of the human drama, a self-styled "democratic spirit" whose self image was largely grounded in the benevolent but patronizing notion that his was a noble love affair with the common people. Appropriately, Walt Whitman was his artistic standard bearer, though the admiration was never greatly appreciated by Whitman. And on the basis of what Phyllis Grosskurth, Symonds' most recent biographer, says about his libidinal excesses, one is led to conclude that Symonds' patriarchal enamourment with the masses may have had more to do with his sexual pursuits and the territory he chose to stalk than it did with his humanitarianism; but, be that as it may, his need to patronize the commonality made it impossible for him to give Pater a fair reading.[59] He could not suspend his presuppositions long enough to see that not only was he not treating Pater fairly, he was, even more damagingly, misinterpreting him.

In 1890, in an essay entitled "Democratic Art. With Special Reference to Walt Whitman," he asked the following questions: "Can we hope that the men who write poems, paint pictures, carve statues, shall enter once again into vital *rapport* with the people . . . the people who are now so far more puissant and important than they ever were before in the world's history? . . . Or is art destined to subside lower and lower into a kind of Byzantine decrepitude, as the toy of a so-called cultivated minority?"[60] Though he did not call specifically for critics as well as creative writers to seek that "vital *rapport*," nevertheless, it is not difficult to imagine where he believed Pater belonged in his calculation. Moreover, there is one section in the essay that stood as a clear, well aimed rebuttal of Pater's argument in "The School of Giorgione" that art should be independent of mere intelligence. Citing as his authority, Whitman's "Democratic Vistas," he noted that democracy requires art that is turbid and "pregnant with sympathetic intelligence of the main issues."[61] To avoid main issues, by which we must assume he meant sociological or political issues, is, therefore, not to have the interests of the people at heart. Again, in another essay, entitled "The Criterion of Art," he recommended that the ultimate criterion for artistic judgment was nothing as vague as how well it approximates the condition of music, as Pater advises, or how well it approximates any other singular medium; but was, instead, the common perception of normal men and women, not insensible either to beauty or to ideas, as to what should be first rate, second rate, or worthless. And the common perception, he added, was not to be confused with simply the judgment of the majority at any one, given time in history. For first rate art, though it must communicate the greatest amount of satisfaction to the greatest number of normal human beings, must do so as well for the greatest length of time.[62]

The problem with Symonds' Benthamite test of the first rate as opposed to the inferior is that, in spite of his repeated concern for the future free development of artistic pursuits, his time-test was locked by his own prejudice into rather typical nineteenth-century judgments. With the haughty assuredness characteristic of so much Victorian art criticism, he assumed that what nineteenth-century European, especially English, taste had stamped as first rate, the twentieth century, from Calais to Calcutta, would merely reaffirm, posting in the natural course of time its own additions to the artistic honor roll. And so he insisted that it followed from his test that the consensus about the greatness of Homer, Virgil, Dante, Shakespeare, and Phidias now amounted to a certainty. Of course, it amounted to a certainty because many Victorian intellectuals, hardly a democratic majority, had sanctioned the composition for posterity of the literary and artistic canon. One wonders if the majority of the populace, even in Victoria's mighty England, actually knew who Phidias was let alone why some members of the Academy claimed greatness for him. Furthermore, Symonds' test, when applied to sculpture, resulted in the surprising conclusion that Bernini was inferior and would not survive the judgment of a trained perception.[63]

His application of this self-conceived deferment to the ordinary as the test and measure of artistic value indicates that he was hopelessly prejudiced in his judgment of Pater and, hence, like Mrs. Pattison and others during the early years of Pater's career who criticized him for not writing history, though less narrowly confined in his assessment, Symonds was also unable to give him a fair reading. Symonds criticized him as undemocratic, an elitist, an over refined dilettante whose theories of art were so limited and narrow that they could benefit none but the slimmest minority. More significantly, he thought that Pater's aestheticism was detrimental to the cause of the propagation of art among the masses. Symonds' vision was so prejudicial that he was blinded to the real intention of Pater's work. For Pater's emphasis, particularly in *The Renaissance*, was directed at a mode of perception—that is, *how* a work of art should be viewed rather than what it should or should not do. And it allowed for a most egalitarian standard of judgment that would give everyone the freedom to find on an individual basis what was most pleasing and satisfying about the work. Symonds could neither comprehend that intention, nor did he have any sympathy with it. He simply did not know what to make of Pater. Publicly, he offered faint praise; privately, the most he could say that when scrutinized does not crumble away like poorly mixed mortar was that Pater gave him the "creeps."

But, ironically, time has exonerated Pater's judgment and Symonds now appears short-sighted, elitist, and premature. For in spite of Symonds' derogations, Pater, at least, had a place in his theories of perception that accommodated Japanese screen painting as well as Raphael's "School of Athens" and that, also, left the final judgment of both up to the tastes of the independent viewer rather than what is often either the obsequious knee-bending of the cultured few or the acquiescent consensus of the trusting but intimidated majority.

CHAPTER II

Well-Intended Reviewers

With George Saintsbury (1845-1933) expressions of approval that were
to form the positive side of Pater's reputation, at least as a prose stylist,
began to take shape. As a student at Oxford, Saintsbury had been caught
up in the "art for art's sake" sentiment of the 'sixties and 'seventies; in
Swinburne, Poe, Gautier, Baudelaire, and Flaubert he found kindred
souls and a cause to champion. He read widely in French literature dealing
with theories of aestheticism. It was therefore quite natural that he should
have taken to Pater. Not only did he know Pater, first meeting him in
person at the Oxford home of Mandell Creighton who was himself quite
interested in aestheticism, but also Saintsbury discovered in Pater another
kindred soul, an English representative of stylistic theories that he had
been attracted to since the 1860's.

He was a journalist, a professional critic, and one of a select body of
professional writers on literature who were transformed into academicians
during the last thirty years of the century, a phenomenon unique to the
period. The list also included William Minto, David Masson, and Edmund
Gosse. Saintsbury was appointed Regius Professor of English at Edinburgh
University in 1895, suceeding Masson, a position he held until 1915.
Prior to his tenure at Edinburgh he had published a distinguished collection of works, including a history of Elizabethan literature (1887) and a
Short History of French Literature (1882). During and after his tenure,
he published a wealth of critical books, articles and reviews: a series of
articles for *Encyclopaedia Britannica* and the *Cambridge History of English Literature*; ten introductions for Ward's *English Poets* series; a *Short
History of English Literature* (1898); a *History of Criticism* (1900-
1904); a *History of English Prosody* (1906-1910); lives of Dryden, Scott,
and Arnold; as well as contributing numerous articles and reviews to
journals and collections. His *Collected Essays and Papers* ran to four
volumes when published in 1923. Stephen Potter in *The Muse in Chains*,
a humorously irreverent and disrespectful accounting of the early develop-

ment of the teaching of English literature, refers to him as the champion, the king, the emperor of the new subject, whose most remarkable characteristic was his ability to conceal his judgments and, consequently, himself. It was a characteristic that Potter calls "personal ghostliness," a characteristic which helps, he adds, "to account for his style, which, since the style is the man and in this case there is no man, is a non-style."[1]

Nevertheless, the man—or his ghost—seems to have read everything and to have acquired an unequalled storehouse of miscellaneous knowledge. Sir Herbert Grierson noted in a personal recollection that it was a point of principle with Saintsbury, following from his great reverence for reading, not to tell his readers much about the contents of any book, lest his comments be substituted for their own efforts.[2] From a modern perspective, however, the result is maddening; his works are monologues, conversations with himself, most of the time. He seems always to be enthusiastic about what he is reading, and the emphasis of his criticism is directed primarily at communicating that enthusiasm. Consequently, he says little of substance, little that is particular or specific about the subject matter or the author. His critiques become little more than a series of effusive generalizations, erudite ramblings, intoxicating impressions. None of it, as John Gross remarks, seems to add up or ultimately to matter much: "sooner or later everyone who has written about him is moved to draw an analogy between his attitude to literature and his vast knowledge of wine. The connoisseur sips, savours, pronounces judgment . . . determined not to let anything interfere with his enjoyment."[3] His enthusiasm and zeal for *all* that was literature is admirable and praiseworthy, but it also seems to have obstructed his ability to discern any measurable difference between the prose of, for instance, Robert Louis Stevenson and that of John Wilson, another Scotchman, but one who wrote earlier in the century. Perhaps, there is no difference, but the reader is unable to make a judgment on the basis of what Saintsbury provides. He fails to explain what they had in common or how they differed. Of Wilson, whose pen name was Christopher North, he simply advanced the claim, unsupported, that as an essayist and critic he had hardly an equal. North's *Noctes Ambrosianae*, a series of table-talk, providing occasion for "wonderfully various digressions," have lasting value as genial and "recreative" literature filled with happy thoughts and happy expressions, an "almost incomparable fulness of life," and a magnificent humor.[4] Happy thoughts, fulness of

38

life, and humor—the major attributes of Wilson's strength as an essayist; and on the basis of those hazy attributes, Saintsbury rested his case for the unequalled talent of John Wilson. Perhaps, Wilson deserved the attention and respect that Saintsbury claims, but without Saintsbury or another literary advocate to provide the argument, he had little hope of receiving it. As well-intended as Saintsbury was in his enthusiasm, he never seems to have realized that future generations of readers might welcome something more substantial than lofty praise for happy thoughts and the fulness of life.

Needless to say, he was not, in the modern sense, a scholar-critic. He disliked, in fact, academic specialization and specialized forms of research. His ultimate philosophy, Gross concludes, was simple: "first read all the books, and then recommend whatever you have enjoyed as forthrightly as possible."[5] But if not an astute critic, in the modern sense, he was a natural as a teacher. He is reported to have been especially good with small groups of honors students.[6] It may well be more efficacious and fair to Saintsbury's reputation to remember him for his pedagogical virtues, for what he said and did to promote the teaching of English literature, a subject then in its infancy, than it is to attempt to find a place for him as a critic. As a teacher, he was somewhat of an innovator for his time. Instead of advising students on *how* a text might be read, particularly, in reaction to English professors whose emphasis for years had been on philology and textual interpretation, often producing little more than the study of footnotes and textual variations, Saintsbury at least tried to get the emphasis shifted to the work, if only to record how one might respond to it. He seems to have believed that the best way for a teacher to interest his students in the text was through the manifestation of interest demonstrated by the teacher himself; that is, the expression of the teacher's impressions— what he experienced as he read. The test of a literary work's applicability to the classroom depended then on the sustained, unrelinquishing nature of the teacher's enthusiasm. In an essay "On the Teaching of English," published in *Athenaeum* in 1920, he acknowledged that annotation was very difficult and serious business; adding, however, that on the subject of its utility in the classroom, "no experienced person who has taught largely will deny that hardly any two class-fellows require exactly the same kind of annotation." He admits that he would rather use "plain texts, at most provided with a biography strictly confined to facts," accompanied by "a most ruthless castigation of mere repetition of professorial or magisterial opinion." Instead of drilling students on footnotes, the immediate object of the teacher of English literature, he argues, should be "to interest the learners in reading, and to show them how to acquire and exercise such interest."[7] Unfortunately, though it had its place in the classroom, the manifestation of interest theory, when applied to his criticism was artificial and shapeless. It did little to effect any real interest in John Wilson, the Scottish essayist, and it proved to be no more successful even when applied to the works of already well-established writers.

Consider, for another example, his essay on Robert Herrick. Published in 1892 as an introduction to an edition of Herrick's poetry, the essay moves toward the lame conclusion that Herrick is "complete," having secured for "poetical representation a most unusual number of interesting subjects." The conclusion is based partly on a section immediately preceding in which he compares Donne with Herrick, citing as the distinctive difference the suggestion that Donne moves in a higher sphere and that Herrick, by contrast, is "smooth and round." After assuring the reader that Herrick's nature had no "bad blood" in it, if but "a slight deficiency of . . . the nobler spirits which transcend the blood," the reader is treated to a humorous, characteristically Saintsburian wine analogy. Saintsbury argues that though Herrick's taste was a little indiscriminate, Herrick nevertheless anticipated the taste of the next generation by having the foresight to detect the excellence of Burgundy wine. The link between his taste for Burgundy wine and his poetry is ingeniously maneuvered. His taste in wine, because it admitted the freedom of experimentation at a time when sack was carrying the day, was a very promiscuous taste indeed, he argues. Hence, the link—it was an indicator of his equally undiscriminating taste in matters of love, to which he was ready to admit anything, and about which, of course, so much of his poetry was written.[8] The analogy suggests that Saintsbury acted, at times, on secret inclinations about people based on the treasured notion that "a man is what he drinks." Consider the possibilities of the Saintsbury wine test being applied to a drinker as prolific as, say, Dylan Thomas. One can only speculate on the insight that study could produce. But, with Saintsbury, we should be grateful for the continual light touches. His genial good cheer, with which he seems to have undertaken his work, is never far from his criticism, no matter how foolish at times it may appear; and that quality of good cheer and gentle humor in his criticism (did he really believe that Herrick's taste for Burgundy was a gauge of his unrestraint?) saves it and continues to make it readable.

But the humor that lifts the Herrick essay is unfortunately absent in the Pater essays; it is equally unfortunate that the vacuity is not. Saintsbury was one of the earliest critics to sing Pater's praises almost unreservedly. His first published acclamation, based on a reading of *The Renaissance*, appeared in 1876 in an essay entitled "Modern English Prose," written for the *Fortnightly Review* at the request of its young editor, John Morley. In the essay, he claims a high ranking among the younger writers for Pater; *The Renaissance* has proven to have an excellence that should be cultivated in the present age, he urges. In particular, Pater's stylistic strength is "the subordinate and yet independent beauty of the sentences when taken separately from the paragraph." Every "word, phrase, clause, sentence and paragraph hold their proper place and dignity."[9] When "Modern English Prose" was reprinted in 1923 in *Collected Essays and Papers*, Saintsbury, older and more critically guarded, included a note intended to soft pedal the exuberance of his youthful claims: that early essay, he cautioned, "was written but a year or two after Mr. Pater's *Renaissance* had definitely sounded the horn for return to ornateness: and therefore may have some interest."[10]

In spite of what seems to be an apology for youthful enthusiasm, his early encomiums on Pater's style in "Modern English Prose" did set a tone that remained consistent throughout all of his following discussions. In 1896, for instance, in *A History of Nineteenth Century Literature (1780-1895)*, he summarized the major points of *The Renaissance*, commented favorably on Pater's refined and guarded hedonism, placed Pater in a tradition that is supposed to have extended from Arnold and Ruskin, and provided an historical survey of Pater's major publications with brief, general, highly impressionistic accompanying comments. He concluded that though Pater is the master of the prose paragraph, he falls short of the poetic grandeur of Sir Thomas Browne, the "phantasmagoric charm" of De Quincey, or the panorama of Ruskin.[11] That same year, 1896, Saintsbury published an essay on Pater in Craik's edition of *English Prose Selections* in which he argued that Pater's prose exemplified the best kind of intellectual savoring of diverse styles, periods, and literary manners; a prose style that he called Corinthian.[12] Other essays and items on Pater followed: in 1906 in *The Bookman*; in 1907 in *The Later Nineteenth Century*, volume twelve of *Periods of European Literature*; and in 1912 in his famous *A History of English Prose Rhythm* in which he noted an amazing sense of "quiet" in Pater's works, reiterated his praise of Pater's care for the paragraph, and claimed for him a place in the literary canon as the father of all turn of the century writers who essay to write delicately.[13]

Although, by the time Saintsbury finished publishing his famous history of criticism in 1904, the prevailing critical trend, following Pater's theory of "appreciation," was to define what made a work different from all other works and to isolate and celebrate that particular strength, Saintsbury's criticism of Pater, though always highly supportive of his style, provided little that advanced any serious critical understanding of his works or his place in the world of modern letters. Pater had been grateful for Saintsbury's support; any support in the light of so much adverse criticism would have been a relief. A. Blyth Webster, in his memoir of Saintsbury, notes that after the publication of "Modern English Prose" in 1876 in *Fortnightly*, Pater wrote to Saintsbury to express "special gratification" for Saintsbury's recognition of his "care for the paragraph."[14] But caring for the paragraph was not going to be enough to guarantee Pater a significant accounting in the future study of English literature. Although Saintsbury's unqualified praise—because he was Saintsbury— helped to produce a general impression, it did not provide any kind of interpretive, critical handle for readers to grasp. Saintsbury's avoidance or, more accurately, his refusal to judge the critical value of an author's work is basically why Herbert Read, early in this century, dismissed his work as vacant criticism. Read contended that Saintsbury really did not write criticism; that his books, instead, were simple surveys of history. Being afraid to judge, Saintsbury was forced to view literature as a refuge from the demands of life, instinctively avoiding writers who dealt with daily human problems. He could not define his hierarchy of values; his thoughts, Read contends, bounce off into vacancy—nobody knows where and, what is more, nobody really cares.[15]

Read is quite right, though his judgment was unnecessarily harsh, stemming to a large extent from Read's own adamantine disposition to favor literature as a criticism of life. But the essence of his reservation about Saintsbury as a critic has since been voiced by others. More recently, for instance, Wendell Harris, writing of the late century critics, noted that because Saintsbury avoided establishing first principles, critical systems, or even metaphysical justifications, it is difficult to get a grip on his mind or to find "any underlying unity in his criticism."[16] The critic's role, as it has come to be viewed regularly in the twentieth century, was not the role of the critic that Saintsbury had envisioned.

In spite of his exuberant praise for Pater and his prose and the favorable general impression of Pater that he created, Saintsbury did not therefore provide any direction for students interested in assessing Pater's primary and lasting contribution to literature. In fact, he may have clouded and damaged Pater's reputation more than he helped it by identifying Pater's aestheticism with his own extreme interpretation of "art for art's sake," specifically his early insistence on the importance of style over subject, a principle that Pater denied but that later critics, regardless, were to claim as fundamental to Pater's and Saintsbury's doctrine. George Levine and William Madden, for example, as recently as 1968 argued that Pater's and Saintsbury's attitudes were similar, that both wished to divorce literature and art from all that made it significant, and that it was Pater's example in the first place which produced the dilettantism of Saintsbury. Herbert Read, earlier, had expressed a similar reservation. There may be some truth to the claim that Saintsbury found his example in Pater; but his reading of Pater was based, judging from what he subsequently wrote, on a very superficial, almost totally stylistically directed assessment of his merit, for which Pater should certainly not be held accountable.[17] Saintsbury could not see, or refused to see, beyond Pater's extravagant diction and exotic turns of phrase. For him, manner was everything; matter counted for little.

In his review of Saintsbury's *Specimens of English Prose Style* for *The Guardian* in 1886, Pater cautioned that if there was a weakness in Saintsbury's view, it was in his "tendency to regard style as a little too independently of matter."[18] Saintsbury envisioned himself as a disciple of Pater and "art for art's sake," but his over insistence on the importance of form as well as his inability to see that aestheticism, particularly as Pater advocated it, was also a philosophy of life, a signal for an open and unrestricted receptivity to new experiences and new ideas, placed him in a position, critically and aesthetically, that was quite distinct from Pater's. His own reputation, fully deserved or otherwise, as a critic who refused to

43

treat literature as anything other than "pure" art, as Dorothy Richardson noted in 1944, was largely responsible for his loss of respect and credibility as a literary critic and historian in the early years of the twentieth century.[19]

For Pater, Saintsbury's efforts in support of his work were inconsequential. And though he was one of the first and most celebrated of Pater's prominent critical proponents, he actually did little more in the final analysis for Pater's reputation than celebrate his care for the paragraph and claim a position for him among those who essay to write delicately. Pater's reputation as a critic merited more assistance than that.

Another of Pater's well-intended supporters was Mrs. Humphry Ward (1851-1920). Like Mrs. Pattison, Mrs. Ward was also part of the Oxford social scene during the early years of Pater's tenure at Brasenose College. She was of the literary nobility. Malcolm Elwin writes that she was the granddaughter of the famous Dr. Thomas Arnold of Rugby, the niece of Matthew Arnold; and adds that it was, to the end of her days, a lineage from which she never recovered.[20] She had lived at Oxford since 1865 when, as a fourteen year old, she moved there with her family. During her adolescent years in Oxford, she socialized with the Pattisons and the T. H. Greens; met George Eliot and G. H. Lewes; listened to Taine lecture; learned to play croquet; and, in general, absorbed the contagious social, cultural, and intellectual atmosphere. She also absorbed the atmosphere of agnosticism that was prevalent as well in certain Oxford circles.

In April 1872, she married Mr. Thomas Humphry Ward, who was also at Brasenose. They lived in Oxford for nine years, until the spring of 1881. Almost immediately opposite to them in Bradmore Road lived Pater and his sisters. She recalls the Oxford reaction in 1873 to the publication of *The Renaissance*. There was a strange sense of beauty in it, she notes. It was entirely aloof from the Christian tradition of Oxford, glorifying "the higher and intenser forms of esthetic pleasure, of 'passion' in the intellectual sense—as against the Christian doctrine of self-denial and renunciation." And even as late in her life as 1918 in *A Writer's Recollections*, she recalls clearly the time when cries of "Neo-paganism" and attempts at persecution were directed at Pater, but were cries which, at that time in his life, left him "unmoved." "In those days," she adds, creating a tone of faded glory, his "mind was still full of revolutionary ferments." And the ferments were "sincere"; no less sincere and "just as much himself, as that later hesitating and wistful return toward Christianity, and Christianity of the Catholic type, which is embodied in *Marius the Epicurean*."[21]

There is a lasting fondness for Pater evident in everything she says and writes about him; but the tone of her recollections during and after the publication of *The Renaissance* consistently hints at an impatience with what she believed Pater had become. There was a change in his attitude of mind with which she seems to have had great sympathy but which she did not approve. Her sense of regret over this change in attitude is emphasized by the obvious relish with which she tells the story of a dinner party at Pater's house during those early years, where a tumult arose because of something he had said to the high church wife of a professor. Pater was being, as she records it, "in some way pressed controversially beyond the point of wisdom" and responded by stating bluntly that "no reasonable person could govern his life by the opinions or actions of a man who died eighteen centuries ago." At which point, she notes, the professor and his wife departed hurriedly in a state of noticeable agitation, adding to her reminiscence, "I look back to them both with the warmest affection."[22] Her affection may have been extended to the offended couple, but in this particular instance her sympathies were squarely with Pater. She was an outspoken critic of fundamental Christian beliefs; in the estimation of some critics, she is to be remembered as a vocal apologist for unbelief. The Pater of the story she recalls in *Recollections* is the Pater "unmoved," standing defiant before the onslaught; he is not the hesitating, melancholic figure of later years whose mood of submissive conciliation, she believed, was expressed "again and again in the . . . pages of *Marius*."[23] Her impatience with the change of mood that she suspected took place in him between *The Renaissance* and the publication of *Marius* is made more clear in her 1885 review of *Marius*.

She begins her review by recalling that *The Renaissance* was a work that represented "an intellectual mood" of high culture, a mood not within the reach of just anybody, but a mood that characterized Pater at that particular time. And though he asked little more in the book than that life be lived with ardor and not apathy, still he was misunderstood; and it was believed by some that the foundation for it all was Epicureanism, pure and simple. Since then, she continues, he has published essays that have revealed "new qualities in the man." But even as late as 1879 in "The Child in the House," his imaginary portrait, his thoughts had not advanced to the point he desired. In *Marius*, however, he found the vehicle that allowed his thoughts "fair play." The novel is a "confession"; its object is to trace the development of a sensitive mind through experiences with various religious and intellectual forces present in Antonine Rome. Eventually, the sensitive hero is overcome by the charm of Christianity. While the novel can be read strictly on a literal level, as a rich story of a speculative and sensitive youth, no reader familiar with Pater's preceding works can fail to see that it is autobiographical. In fact, she claims, Marius begins his pilgrimage with principles clearly presented in the "Conclusion" to *The Renaissance*. But he soon changes; his youthful exuberance fades and the man begins to see that systems that find their center in "moments" leave most of life untouched. She concludes that "although the fundamental argument is really the same as that on which Mr. Pater based a general view of life twelve years ago, the practical advance in position . . . is considerable."[24]

Her words are chosen with care. Given the way her argument evolves in the review, one would expect at this point, some conventional observation about the maturity of Pater's vision or the perspicuity of his thought as he finally recognizes and attains to the qualities preliminary to an acceptance of the legitimacy of belief. But, instead, her conclusion is that he made a "practical advance in position." The "practical advance" she refers to is described further as an enlargement of experience that "tends to coalesce and join hands with other powers." And so, she writes, after arguing in *The Renaissance* against any curtailment of any kind of experience for the sake of "some abstract morality," Pater now argues *for* that morality, "not because of any absolute virtue or authority inherent in it, but because practically obedience is a source of pleasure and quickened faculty to the individual." At this point in her review, what becomes clear is that in spite of a tone of generous sympathy with Pater, the review is, in large measure, unfavorable. But she is remarkably cautious in her criticism.

Pater's major weakness, she claims, is the application of his aesthetic principles to religion—specifically, Christianity. His argument, she suggests, is that just as acceptance of the moral order enriches and widens experience so too does "acquiescence in the religious order, which a man finds about him." It too opens for him new feelings, new sensations, new "moments." The argument is really quite common, she remarks; surprisingly, much more common than is generally admitted. " 'Submit,' it seems

46

to say, 'to the religious order about you, accept the common beliefs, or at least behave as if you accepted them. . . . surrender your feeling, while still maintaining the intellectual citadel intact; pray, weep, dream with the majority while you think with the elect; only so will you obtain from life all it has to give. . . ."[25]

The surrender of feelings, she contends, is a peculiarly modern idea with great appeal; but with another body of intellectuals who seem not to need religion so strongly, it never will have any hope of success. The reason? And here one must remember that she is directing her comments at Pater. Submission and the surrender of feelings will not affect some intellectuals because "they regard it as involving the betrayal of a worship dearer to them than the worship of beauty or consolation, and the surrender of something more precious to them than any of those delicate emotional joys, which feeling, divorced from truth, for the sense of reality, has to offer." And to this temper of mind—Pater's temper of mind, to be sure —she compares that of A. H. Clough. Clough's may also be a mood of submission, but it is "heroic submission to the limitations of life and mind which inspired all his verse," his determination "to seek no personal ease or relief at the expense of truth, and to put no fairy tales knowingly into the place which belongs to realities."[26] His is surely a nobler counsel of perfection. Her final word on *Marius* is that, as a novel, it remains a delight to read; one finds in it a wealth of reflection. Her quarrel is not with the imaginative qualities of the novel; it is with what she believes the novel implies about the relationship between intellectual honesty and the "practical advances" and convenience one secures through the surrender of feeling, divorced from truth. Pater finally had chosen personal ease, she suggests; this uncommon man had surrendered his feelings and submitted to common beliefs—all at the expense of truth. In doing so, he betrayed a worship dearer than the worship of consolation.[27]

Her judgment was harsh; and though he thanked her for the review, acknowledging her objections, in a letter he sent to her on June 2, 1885, it still must have unsettled him.[28] *Marius* was not the only piece of evidence upon which she based her case. She had other reason to believe that Pater had weakened and compromised himself. In 1918 in *Recollections*, she writes of the years prior to the publication of *Marius*. She notes that Edmund Gosse, in the biographical sketch of Pater contributed in 1917 to the *Dictionary of National Biography*, said that before 1870

Pater had gradually relinquished *all* belief in Christianity. He leaves it there, she adds. What Gosse did not see was that though Pater never returned to Christianity in the orthodox, intellectual sense, "his heart returned to it." To emphasize the point, she cites an incident she recalls from the late 1870's: she had said to Pater that "orthodoxy could not possibly maintain itself long against its assailants, especially from the historical and literary camps, and that we should live to see it break down." To which Pater, noticeably troubled, disagreed, responding, " 'There are such mysterious things. Take that saying, 'Come unto me, all ye that are weary and heavy-laden.' How can you explain that? There is a mystery in it—something supernatural.' "[29] She must have looked for the text. Unable to find it, she recalls in retrospect that she would have liked to have said to him, "the words you quote are in all probability from a lost Wisdom book; there are very close analogies in Proverbs and in the Apocrypha. They are a fragment without a context." But, she adds, even such a controvertible reply would not have "affected the mood in Pater, of which this conversation gave me my first glimpse, and which is expressed again and again in . . . *Marius.*"[30] And so, what she believed was a first glimpse of Pater's mood of submission to orthodoxy came to her in the late 'seventies, some years before the appearance of *Marius*. When *Marius* did appear, she was prepared for a testament of faith, a reaffirmation of his earlier sentiments.

Her review was published in the June 1885 issue of *Macmillan's Magazine*. Pater did not wait long to respond. That very month he wrote to her that her objections were "full of import and interest," the chief of which, he added, he would deal with before long.[31] Six months later, after having received from her as a Christmas gift a copy of her newly published translation of Henri-Frédéric Amiel's *Journal Intime*, he wrote a letter of thanks, dated 23 December 1885, in which, intentionally or not, he answered in part, one of her earlier objections. In the review she had said that the major weakness of the novel was in Pater's attempt to show that aesthetic principles that could be applied to morals could just as easily be applied to Christianity.[32] In the letter, Pater responded by noting that he saw no disparity between morals and the Christian religion, that "the supposed facts on which Christianity rests, utterly incapable as they have become of any ordinary test, seem to me matters of very much the same sort of assent we give to any assumption, in the strict and ultimate sense, moral."[33] Later, in *Recollections*, she recalls his response to her translation of the *Journal*, and she reprints the passage from the letter of 23 December that included the preceding quotation, "a passage," she remarks, "of considerable interest as throwing light upon the inner mind of one of the ... most important influences of the nineteenth century. Certainly there is no sign in it," she adds, "on Mr. Pater's part, of 'dropping Christianity'; very much the contrary."[34] And so, added to her memory of that first glimpse of Pater's mood of submission to orthodoxy in the 'seventies, and to her interpretation of *Marius* in 1885 as a "practical advance" on that position, was Pater's response to *Amiel's Journal*.

But she exaggerated the degree of his emotional commitment to Christianity, even though she admits early in the review that Marius' death is surrounded by ambiguity and that "apparently, he remains intellectually free."[35] It is the word "apparently" that carries the weight of the sentence, for in the remaining pages of the review she constructs a case *for* submission and "acquiescence in the religious order" for those who represent an order of mind for whom the need to surrender the emotions, the feelings, is irresistible. But whose suspected surrender, in fact, did she have in mind —Marius' or Pater's? At the end of the novel, Marius is still seeking the elusive Ideal; there is no clear indication of a formal conversion or surrender to Christianity.

She had contended that Pater was arguing from feelings and emotions in *Marius*; the implication was that he had surrendered to orthodoxy. On 17 March 1886, three months after receiving his copy of her translation of *Amiel's Journal*, he published his review of it in *The Guardian*. Again, he attempted to clarify his position for her. Amiel, he writes, was a man divided, of two minds: there was the " 'man of disillusion,' " of negation, and the man of creativity who took the mood of negation into his service and made the most positive use of whatever "evidence" was available to him. At times, with Amiel, he adds, "we feel that there has been ... an intellectual effort to get at the secret ... to *define* feeling." He realized that artistic or literary construction rested " 'upon feeling, instinct, and,' alas! also, 'upon will.' " But something kept him back from "commensurate production"—"a cause purely intellectual." Amiel failed to realize that "old-fashioned Christianity is itself but the proper historic development of the true 'essence' of the New Testament." He also failed "to see the equally probable evidence there is for the beliefs, the peculiar directions of men's

49

hopes, which . . . bring them into connection with . . . the venerable institutions of the past—with the lives of the saints." Because he failed to see the historic significance and appeal of the church as a cultural and civilizing phenomenon, he got no further "than the glacial condition of rationalistic Geneva." We are left with "only the *Journal*," Pater concludes; watching in it, the two minds and "observing how the one might have ascertained and corrected the shortcomings of the other."[36] It is a condition that did not, by contrast, impede the development and the more open-minded vision of his own Marius. Pater's response to Amiel's dilemma was hardly that of the unquestioning believer who had surrendered his feelings; it was, instead, the carefully reasoned argument of a liberal thinker, feeling the effects, particularly on the vision of history, of the teachings of Positivism.

Two years later, on 28 March 1888, in his review of her novel, *Robert Elsmere* for the *Guardian*, he had another opportunity to respond to her claims and to clarify his position. Robert Elsmere, he writes, represents "a large class of minds which cannot be sure that the sacred story is true. . . . But then," he adds, "there is also a large class of minds which cannot be sure it is false. . . . For their part, they make allowances in their scheme of life for a great possibility, and with some of them that bare concession of possibility . . . becomes the most important fact in the world. . . . The question of the day is not between one and another of these, but in another sort of opposition, as well defined by Mrs. Ward herself, between—'two estimates of life—the estimate which is the offspring of the scientific spirit, and which is for ever making the visible world fairer and more desirable in mortal eyes; and the estimate of Saint Augustine.' "[37] Pater was obviously on the side of the former. *Robert Elsmere* argued the position that Christianity could survive as an ethical ideal solely—devoid of its mystical and miraculous trappings. Pater disagreed. To demythologize the Christ figure and to strip the church of its miraculous elements, he argues, is to rob the whole ancient story of its artistic power and to muzzle forever the grand, time-honored oratory that it has produced.

Pater's review of *Robert Elsmere* was a cautious warning to those who would overlook the diversity of the "problem" and interpret the "religious question" oversimply, as a conflict between illiberal denunciation, on one hand, and the unyielding spirit of orthodoxy, on the other. Pater's position was finally that of a fair and honest and admittedly receptive skeptic, a man imbued, himself, with the scientific spirit.

From the outset, it was unreasonable of Mrs. Ward to expect a theologically reasoned argument that would appeal to the intellect from Pater and then to fault him for not providing it. Pater was true to his feelings about the value of everything that had ever interested mankind—which for a disposition like his had to account for more than just intellect. It was that particular "truth" that he tried, after *Marius* had so obviously dismayed her, to clarify in his reviews of *Amiel's Journal* and of *Robert Elsmere*. For *Marius* and the subsequent reviews were attempts to explain his open-minded skepticism. His arguments reaffirmed his earlier position, explained in the "Conclusion" to *The Renaissance*, in particular, on the relativity of all that can be known and understood—a position that Mrs. Ward had associated with his life during the years prior to the publication of *Renaissance*, before he began what she called his wistful and hesitating return to dogma. The most salient point that Pater may well have been trying to make in the reviews was that, in spite of what she suggested in her review of *Marius*, his position on the relative nature of all knowledge had not changed; most certainly, it had not changed in the direction she believed. Though publicly he may have been attempting to establish a more harmonious relationship with the orthodox during the years following the publication of *The Renaissance*, his convictions, at least about dogmatic assertions, had not varied. As late as *Plato and Platonism*, the last volume he published before his death, he was still arguing at length for the contingency of truth, the all-informing principle of flux, and the need for the life-long pursuit of the elusive Ideal.[38]

Mrs. Ward had made up her mind by 1885 about his submissive surrender. And, judging from her observations on him as late as 1918 in *Recollections*, she appears not to have altered her opinion in the slightest. The tenacity with which she maintained her judgment is amazing. She was convinced that Pater had compromised himself. By contrast, her own Robert Elsmere prevailed to the end without compromise, especially the type of compromise she had detected in *Marius*. It seems to me significant that she began work on *Robert Elsmere* in the early summer of 1885, after she had finished translating *Amiel's Journal*; at the time, she had just finished reading and reviewing *Marius* as well, for the review appeared in June. It is hard not to believe that *Marius* had some slight influence on her thought as she formulated the early plans for *Robert Elsmere*. Perhaps, she intended it as something of a response. But be that as it may, what is most telling about all of her observations, early and late, on his hesitating turn of mind during the years prior to the publication of *Marius* is the distinct possibility that she may have had her mind made up about his "surrender" even before the novel and her subsequent review appeared. Her predisposition is clearly evident in her *Recollections*. She had expected *Marius* to be a wistful and hesitating return to Christianity, and it was as a wistful and hesitating return to Christianity that she reviewed it. Her own *Robert Elsmere*, by contrast, was to be a testament to steadfastness. It was created with the assumption in mind that doubt necessitated departure; to waver and yet remain was cowardice.

No other review published subsequent to the first appearance of *Marius* argued for Pater's melancholic surrender with nearly as much force as Mrs. Ward's.[39] Her review provided a positive and ready made argument for those friends and critics—especially the avowedly Christian ones— who had expected him, after the publication of *The Renaissance* in 1873, to provide his public eventually with a redeeming statement of faith and who now welcomed the novel as a proper corrective, a contrite apology, for his earlier heterodoxy. In spite of the novel's fine-pointed ambiguity, her review encouraged them in the belief that *Marius* was Pater's apologia. What continues to stand out, however, as the inescapable irony is the fact that this tailored argument for Pater's return to the fold should have come from a critic of Christian orthodoxy as outspoken and vocally agnostic as Mrs. Ward.

Other critics, later in the age, were to echo the contention that Pater made his commitment to the faith in *Marius*. In January 1887, an anonymous reviewer for the *Edinburgh Review* commended the novel's "healthy growth" towards Christianity; later, in 1896, a reviewer for *British Weekly*, in an essay on Pater's theology, concluded that his reviews of Mrs. Ward's *Robert Elsmere* and *Amiel's Journal* provided the "proof" that he was a "professed believer in Christ"; another reviewer, that same year, suggested in *Athenaeum* that, owing to its similarities to *Marius*, if *Gaston de Latour*, Pater's unfinished romance, had indeed been finished, it would have shown how skepticism like Montaigne's is "subdued and overcome by the spirit" of Christianity. In 1897, only three years after Pater's death, Stanley Addelshaw, writing in the *Gentleman's Magazine*, noted that Pater's earlier "Pagan" ideas, expressed in *The Renaissance*, had become in *Marius*—"actually Christian." For some, obviously, Pater's conversion had become a fact by that time; and, of course, Pater was no longer alive to provide any challenge to the claim.[40] Even A. C. Benson was later to suggest that if Pater had decided to prolong Marius' progress beyond his threshold attraction to Christian ritual, Marius would have become a professed Christian—Benson was that certain of Pater's sympathies.[41] Pater himself, in a letter to Vernon Lee, written in July 1883, two years before *Marius* appeared, had admitted that he believed that there was a "sort of religious phase possible for the modern mind" and that his "main object" in *Marius* was to describe the conditions of that phase.[42] But assenting to the allurement of a phase of religious belief was hardly tantamount to a total confession of faith. At the very least, however, the appearance of *Marius* and responses to it such as Mrs. Ward's, the irony of her position aside, aided in significantly altering the hedonistic image that many critics and reviewers had created for him after the appearance of the reputedly pagan *Renaissance*.

Pater and Mrs. Ward remained friends throughout his life. D. S. MacColl remembered that in later years, when Pater lived in Earl's Terrace in London, the Humphry Wards were regularly among his dinner guests.[43] And Mrs. Ward, as late as 1892, when *The History of David Grieve* was published, recalled that amidst all of the hostile reactions to the novel came a comforting word from Pater who wrote and told her that the novel had all of the force of *Robert Elsmere* at work in it, "with perhaps a mellower kind of art—a more matured power of blending disparate literary gifts in one."[44] He was obviously fond of her, and she seems to have admired him, in spite of her feelings about his religious surrender. But she did little to promote his reputation as a critic or man of letters with anything particularly significant to offer. If anything, she added to the confusion already resulting from digressive, circuitous questions about his religious character. What neither she nor the other critics who focused their attention on his commitment, or lack of it, to Christianity could see was that he was dealing with subject areas in his criticism that far outweighed in importance the question of how firmly or in what he did or did not believe. But the Victorians, even many of the late Victorians, seem to have been preoccupied with matters of faith and religiosity. And though the concerns were appropriate for the times, given the ongoing conflict between science and religion, they provide little that one can draw from when attempting to find a place for Pater as a critic with something specific to say to twentieth-century readers for whom religious disputes generally merit minor consideration, if considered at all.

As Pater approached the twentieth century, there were few critics, even the ones on his side, who could offer any practical, well-founded reasons for keeping his works in circulation. And Edmund Gosse, though another good friend, was no exception. Gosse (1849-1928) and Saintsbury were both prominent late century men of letters, and both have survived perhaps more as academic journalists, belletristic personalities representing a splendidly respectable, if dusty, tradition of criticism, than on the strength of anything critically formative. Though Saintsbury was better prepared as a student of literature than Gosse, both wrote firmly in the biographical tradition of Sainte-Beuve; but particularly in the case of Gosse, biography too frequently turned to gossip. He was a superficial and careless scholar, admittedly interested more in the personality of the author than in his works, a predisposition that seems harmless enough, but one that, ironically, caused him considerable difficulty.[45]

In 1880, he applied for the Clark Lectureship at Cambridge and was elected. His first set of lectures was published by the Cambridge University Press in 1885 under the title, *From Shakespeare to Pope: An Inquiry into the Causes and Phenomena of the Rise of Classical Poetry in England.* Waiting for its appearance was the less successful academic aspirant, John Churton Collins.

Collins was the symbol of academic frustration—the classical example of the qualified but always unsuccessful candidate. He was turned down by Oxford for the Merton Professorship in 1885, after having campaigned tirelessly for years for the establishment of a chair of English language and literature at Oxford. He was acknowledged to have been the most successful of the extension lecturers, widely published; and he was eminently qualified for the position. Ten years later, he was passed by again for the Merton Professorship of Literature. Cambridge was not interested in him, and so he finally had to settle for a Chair at the University of Birmingham and was probably better off for it in the long run. But Collins felt that he had been sold down the river by the academic politicians, and he had a volcanic and vindictive temper. He also had the nimble agility and holding power of an enraged bull terrier. And when the opportunity arose, he demolished Gosse. The fact that Gosse, without academic credentials, had been appointed Clark Lecturer must have set Collins back initially. And so, in 1885, when Gosse published *From Shakespeare to Pope*, Collins seized the advantage and pilloried him for his errors in *Quarterly Review*. At the time, Collins was only a year removed from the sting of his Oxford defeat and not yet recovered. It is generally agreed that Collins was unnecessarily harsh and exacting in his criticism (Tennyson compared him to a louse wandering on the locks of literature); but he was absolutely right about Gosse's careless and shoddy workmanship. The fact is that Gosse had probably never even looked at some of the works he included in his survey; he discussed Sir Philip Sidney's *Arcadia* and James Harington's *Oceana*, for instance, as poems instead of prose pieces, having confused James Harington the prosaist, born in 1611, with John Harington the poet and translator of Ariosto's *Orlando Furioso*, born in 1561. Minor points, perhaps, as some have argued in Gosse's defense, but certainly the type of mistakes that could seriously shake one's confidence in his authority.

From Shakespeare to Pope was not to be his only literary misfire. His *Life of Congreve*, as well, published in 1888, was constructed on considerable erroneous data. Malcolm Elwin claims that for the *Congreve* he also failed to look at important contemporary accounts. The irony, however, is that Gosse apparently did not have any great attraction to Congreve in the first place and only chose to write the book because he wanted to establish his credentials as a Restoration specialist. Ten years after the *Congreve*, in 1898, Collins was again attacking Gosse for his *Short History of Modern English Literature*. Grudgingly acknowledging Gosse's sympathy for literature and his impressive general knowledge, Collins pointed out that what irritated him most, however, aside from Gosse's shaky inferences and unsound generalizations, was "the habitual employment of phraseology so vague and indeterminate" that it was difficult to submit what is conveyed to any positive test.[46] Collins was again correct in his estimation of Gosse's highly questionable phraseology. It was a caution that other critics, over the years, also raised; and it is a caution that one must keep in mind when assessing the value of what Gosse had to say about Pater as well as any other literary figure he treated.

One argument has it that Gosse was so tediously concerned with good taste, propriety and correctness that he intentionally avoided passing judgments on the meaning or the value of any work, judgments, that is, that would require any kind of specificity or determinateness. He became, as a result, a critic of personality who set out to study the *process* by which the writer's mind worked in order to discover the inspirations that lay at the root of his vision.[47] Another argument has it that he was an extremely ambitious and fashion-conscious opportunist who so wanted to be counted among literary talents that he courted their favor indiscriminately, always admiring what he was supposed to admire, and was inclined, consequently, to obscure the truth if he believed its publication would adversely affect his own reputation.[48]

The pounding he took from Collins may have kept him from achieving any large success in the scholarly world, but it did not seem to get in the way of his popularity in society. Throughout the 'nineties he was in demand in the after dinner circuit and was a highly successful literary lecturer as well. But it was not until well into the twentieth century, in his old age, that he managed to establish himself as a trustworthy literary source. By then the Collins stigma had been forgotten or judged irrelevant (Collins had died in 1908); Gosse was reviewing books for the prestigious *Sunday Times*; and a new generation of readers, as Elwin notes, sat at his feet, eager to listen to entertaining gossip about all of the great literary figures, now dead, from the one man who had survived to draw his breath willingly, irrespective of circumstances, to tell the old stories. And who now could contradict him? His years, Elwin suggests, "procured him a reputation which must have aroused uproarious laughter among contemporaries across the Styx."[49]

Gosse was a johnny-come-lately to the world of letters. He had grown up in a strict religious household and as a solemn and ingenuous little boy had had the example of his piously oppressive, Bible-pounding father always before him. The family was deeply suspicious of secular involvements of all types, particularly ones artistic. But at seventeen, Gosse was rescued and found himself working, though poorly paid, at the British Museum. At some point he became dedicated to the task of making himself a prosperous and renowned literary success, a respected man of letters. He had the instincts of a collector; his greatest asset seems to have been his ability to cultivate people with prestigious literary connections. And so began his career as a professional investor in literary greatness, a collector of famous people. As early as 1867, he had set his enterprising sights on

Swinburne; later, he incorporated, as well, the figures of Stevenson and Donne.

As a maker of reputations he was for his time largely successful, and there is still a need for a careful assessment of his impact on the development of the academic literary canon during those years. As a critic with anything substantial to say, however, he was largely ineffectual, dealing mainly, as Collins warned, in platitudes and circumspect generalizations, cautiously wary not to say anything that had the potential of backfiring on him and jeopardizing his hard-won position as a respected, influential man of letters. Consequently, in his 1894 portrait of Pater published in *Contemporary Review*, the reader is treated to what appear to be harmless judgments; but which, in fact, added to the impression of Pater as some kind of languishing literary oddball, an impression that had survived at least since the time of Mallock's devastating Mr. Rose portrait and which was taking on additional significance as Pater became increasingly more closely associated during the 'nineties with the well publicized vagaries of the aesthetic movement. The general tone of the portrait is favorable and Pater's reputation certainly did not suffer at the time from what appears to be a positive endorsement from the highly influential Gosse, but it is what Gosse fails to say and the impression of Pater at work and play that he creates in the portrait that is devastating—and devastatingly funny as well.

It begins with Gosse's acknowledgement that his focus is limited to Pater's life. The merits of his style and the effect he had on his age must be left for future critics to rescue. The statement in itself is revealing since it indicates that Gosse must have had reservations as late as 1894 about the status of Pater's reputation. It was, as well, that same concern that he seems to be addressing when he claims that this portrait will now present the "facts" about "the author of *Marius*, so oddly travestied at the moment of his death." And although it is a commendable effort in many ways to clear the biographical record on Pater, Gosse's notion of "facts" is so enthusiastically broad and colored by his own concept of himself as the oracle of the arcane, loaded with all those personal and private tid-bits, that what he finally succeeds in doing, obviously unintentionally, is creating an impression of Pater as some kind of cross between a gnomish literary cave dweller and a puckish wombat.

There was a certain dimension to Pater's writing habits that Gosse unfortunately speaks of in subterranean metaphors; the result is amusing, to say the least: "If we take these symbols of a mountain-stream or of a fountain for other prose-writers who have won the ear of the public with little effort, then for Pater the appropriate image seems the artesian well, to reach the contents of which, strata of impermeable clay must be laboriously bored." Gosse is here speaking of Pater's style; his thesis is that Pater wanted to be a poet in prose, not bound by rules but with a free hand to experiment. And he adds again, on the subject of Pater's style: "It was not that there was any lack of material there, nor any doubt about the form it must take when it emerged, but that it was so miraculously deep down and hard to reach." Writing was agony to Pater, he concludes; and anyone with less fortitude would have given up. The amazing effort expended over the early pages of *Marius*, he likens, extending the subterranean coloring, to "the toil as at a deep petroleum well when the oil refuses to flow." And then, in less effluent but equally exuberant fashion, he relates the, by now, classical story about Pater's "little squares" —how he would surround himself with those little squares of paper, like the pieces of a great puzzle, characteristically waiting for the right "moment" to come when the proper square "would serve as monitor or as a guide." It is little wonder, he concludes, that certain disadvantages accompanied his style: "it is not possible to work in this way, with a cold hammer, and yet to avoid a certain deadness and slipperiness of surface." But Pater had wanted to be a prose-poet, and though verse will bear the endless labor of the file, prose should not be subjected to it.[50]

And what long sentences Pater writes, Gosse continues; "broken-backed with having had to bear too heavy a burden of allusion and illustration." But, in spite of its oddities, it was his style that helped give the man his singularity. It was the natural development of his highly "self-centred" personality. He did not read his contemporaries, Gosse claims, and it may have been to his advantage if he had, for "his own writing might have grown a little simpler and a little more supple if he had had the fortitude to come down and fight among his fellows."[51] Earlier, while discussing Pater's reclusiveness, he had claimed that if Pater had lived longer, he probably would have taken orders and a small college living in the country —hardly a "fact" but a most salient commentary on what Gosse probably thought Pater best suited for.[52]

The impression of Pater that Gosse succeeds in conveying is antedi-luvian; Pater emerges as some type of literary laborer among the mole people, a slogger toiling away in a dark, confined fortress beneath the earth. Amusing and entertaining, but hardly the best one could do, especially as a good friend, for his image.

The impression becomes even more amusing when Gosse decides to shift his metaphorical center from the subterranean depths to the zoo in order to describe Pater's "childishness." There are certain animals, similar to wombats or armadillos, "which sit all day immovable and humped up among the riot of their fellows, and which, when all the rest of the mena-gerie is asleep, steal out upon their slip of greensward and play the wildest pranks in the light of the moon." Just such a creature was Pater. Gosse employs this strange and unfortunate analogy as a warning for those who would make Pater out to be too much of the "solemn pundit of aesthetics," without any regard for his great sense of humor. And then, moving from the unfortunate to the truly maladroit, he adds the amusing tid-bit that it was that same sense of the playful that prompted Pater to invent imaginary characters; in particular, an imaginary group of relatives that, eventually, after having talked of them for so long, Pater began to believe were real.[53]

Earlier, Gosse acknowledged his debt to Pater's sisters for the biographi-cal information upon which he based much of the portrait; and the sisters eventually released the "Pascal" manuscript, the essay that Pater was working on when he died, to Gosse for publication. They thought that highly of him. He is also supposed to have been very helpful to the sisters, aiding them with their financial problems after Pater's death.[54] But it is remarkable that the relationship between Gosse and the Pater sisters should have remained so firm for so long, especially when he had just produced a portrait of their recently deceased brother depicting him as some kind of humped-up armadillo who believed that imaginary people were real. Perhaps, they were just trusting and not given to reading very closely.

But colossal exaggerations and the creation of bizarre metaphors were part of Gosse's critical style; he had decided earlier, in 1885, during his visit to Walt Whitman's home in New Jersey, that Whitman's coarse simplicity made him non-human, something akin to "the condition of protoplasm"—an "expanse of crystallisable substances, waiting for the structural change."[55] In 1893, while reviewing Pater's *Plato and Platonism*, he had noted that Pater was an important literary figure of the period, largely because of his personal writing style. It was so personal and so definite, in fact, that "if he now wrote a book on Chinese Pagodas, or on the Habits of the Water-rat, those people who have always read him would devoutly read him still. And they would insist, his volume must not be snatched from them on the pretence that it was either a contribution to architecture or to zoology."[56] The thought must have comforted Pater, who was still alive at the time. The strength of *Plato and Platonism*, Gosse added, is found where the strength of most of Pater's efforts is to be found—in beginnings and endings; for "Mr. Pater is more fascinating as a writer when he is approaching or quitting a subject than when the subject is definitely before him."[57] His final word on Pater's *Plato* is that no one can read the study without perceiving how "exquisite" literary criticism can be in the right hands.[58]

Pater appears, by nature, to have been a very tolerant man; he and Gosse had a long lasting friendship. Gosse first saw Pater in 1871 when Pater and Swinburne dismounted from a cab in front of Rossetti's door in Cheyne Walk. It was not until 1873, however, that he was finally introduced to Pater in William Bell Scott's studio. Early in 1874, he began to visit him with some frequency, and they seem to have remained friends until Pater's death in 1894. In all fairness, Gosse's 1894 portrait, published only a few months after Pater died, has provided scholars with much valuable biographical information, especially since there is a lamentable scarcity of important biographical information on Pater. Along with a score of anecdotes and pertinent information about Pater's family and his personal characteristics, Gosse has provided information on his little known plan to publish a series of studies on French ecclesiastical towns (his essays on Amiens and Vézelay were part of the projected series); the unique theory that he suppressed the "Conclusion" to *The Renaissance* because he was upset with the persistence with which the newspapers attributed to him all sorts of "aesthetic" extravagances; a description of his writing process; the famous story of the student named "Sanctuary," whose name Pater is reported to have found so appealing, a story that Gosse probably heard originally from Mandell Creighton, and many more.[59]

As a biographical source, Gosse has proven to be important; but as an influence on the development of Pater's literary and critical reputation he offered little that helped. If anything, he made Pater out to be even more eccentric than he was. Henry James, in a letter written to Gosse in 1894, in response to the portrait of Pater, praised him for the information he provided on Pater's personal history but regretted that Pater still remained "curiously negative and faintly-grey." The personal history, though important, James chided, should be less important in time than Pater's style, his genius, for he had the good fortune "to have taken it out all, wholly, exclusively, with the pen . . . and absolutely not at all with the person."[60] But whatever it was specifically that his pen had accomplished still remained unclear. And Gosse did not help to clear any of it up. In fact, summarizing the critical observations that he made on Pater and particularly on his writing style over the years, one is left with the distinct impression that Gosse may have had serious reservations about Pater as a stylist and preferred to leave it as gray as James had thought— in which case, the grayness would have more to do with Gosse's refusal to judge and take the consequent risk of threatening his position than it did with any ambiquity associated with Pater directly, as stylist or anything else. Gosse may have believed that Pater was not a critic of the first rank— and if not, then what was there about him that he could recommend?

They were friends, good friends; and Gosse must have felt a great deal of loyalty to his memory, as well as to his sisters. Havelock Ellis, as early as 1885, had already passed judgment on Pater as, at best, a second rate critic.[61] In 1897, only three years after the portrait, Gosse finally felt secure enough to lift his head from the sand and totteringly offered the qualification in his *Short History of Modern English Literature* that though Pater's fame had been "rising by leaps and bounds" since his death because of the high quality attached to his prose style, it now seemed appropriate to sober that enthusiasm with the counter-thought that there was really "something heavy, almost pulpy, in his soft magnificence of style" and it should not be "ignorantly imitated," adding the judgment that his greatest influence was probably the result of the "elevated hedonism of his youth."[62] He had concluded the 1894 portrait by noting that "Pater, as a human being," because of the lack of biographical information, would "grow more and more shadowy"; but as a writer whose polished work was already a classic of English literature, he would "be remembered among the writers of this age when all but a few are forgotten."[63] We must take him at his word; he must have believed that —at least in 1894.

But the impression he finally leaves is as vague as his writing style. How much more he would have done to guarantee Pater's survival, providing he even believed in it, if he had given to posterity, along with the biographical data, something more substantive with which to place and evaluate Pater than a series of extravagant and turgid impressions. The value in reading Gosse on Pater, or Gosse on anybody, for that matter, is in the humor that one finds there. It guarantees Gosse a place as one of the most readable, because he is one of the most entertaining, of all the late century critics.

CHAPTER III

John Morley:
The Positive Turn of Mind

"An actively stirred generation craves a doctrine"
(Morley on "Mr. Pater's Essays")

In spite of influential support from certain highly respected critical quarters, Pater nevertheless approached the twentieth century with a very ill-defined place in the literary hierarchy. Among his most celebrated supporters, Saintsbury had said little that could recommend him as anything more than a careful stylist, particularly good with the paragraph; Gosse, in his purposely vague and indeterminate way, succeeded mainly in adding to the impression that Pater was some kind of an eccentric literary mole; Mrs. Ward had inadvertently done much to remove the stigma of paganism and immorality that seemed to surround him, but she did little to provide any direction that later critics could follow when attempting to assess his place in the world of letters. Of the influential early critics who passed judgment on Pater's essays, the only one who made a serious and substantial effort to place him in the context of Victorian intellectual thought was John Morley (1838-1923), journalist, editor, critic, politician, and statesman—the man Basil Willey lauded in 1956 as "an eminent pioneer" in the history of opinion.[1]

As the young editor of the *Fortnightly Review* during the years 1867 to 1882, Morley was a dedicated, vocal advocate of scientism, liberalism, and Positivist thought. In his highly favorable review of *The Renaissance* in 1873, he approached Pater as a kindred Positivist spirit in the conflict then being aired in the pages of the *Fortnightly* against absolutism and orthodoxy. He had earlier read and accepted for publication in the *Fortnightly* four of the original essays that Pater later included in the first edition of *The Renaissance*. And so it is probably safe to assume that he was predisposed favorably to the book when it was finally published. But one must be cautious about reading too much into Morley's interest in Pater; for, as Edward Alexander recently cautioned, Morley assuredly never persuaded himself that Pater actually was a committed Positivist. Nevertheless, he realized that, like himself, Pater was aware of changed intellectual circumstances within which artists were now obliged to function; and that Pater, though with different ends in mind than the Positivists, "used the historical method to show that all institutions and beliefs were only 'right' and 'true' for their particular periods, not absolutely and eternally."[2] Not only did they share a common feeling for Positivism during those years but they also had in common a sensitivity to the value of continental European thought, and a propensity for French writers, particularly Victor Hugo. These specific connections will be discussed at length below. For the present, it is well to remember that, all things considered, Morley's favorable treatment of Pater at the time was much more than just token support for a developing young writer. Morley was predisposed to the intellectual position that he believed Pater was assuming in the essays. And his interest in Pater's writings did not end with the publication of *The Renaissance*. Before he finally terminated his career as an editor to enter politics, Morley had published nine more of Pater's essays.

It is to Morley's credit that he saw in Pater's work what no other critic at the time saw. But then Morley was incisive, a critic's critic, and it is an unfortunate oversight that he has been denied his place in the literary canon among other prominent literary critics of the Victorian age. Basil Willey claimed for him a position in the literary and intellectual forefront of the times alongside Leslie Stephen and Matthew Arnold.[3] Mrs. Ward admitted to great trust in his judgment and noted that she thought he had the somber intensity of a prophet.[4] The praise was merited.

For the times, Morley wrote singularly unusual and penetrating reviews, unlike the learned gossip of so many of his literary peers. His famous review of Swinburne's *Poems and Ballads* in 1866 is an example. Though it is usually misrepresented as proof of how successfully Swinburne had shocked the Victorian bourgeoisie, it also succeeds in presenting a case in support of poetic license and freedom in the choice of subject matter, regardless of public sentiment. The problem with the review is that the frantic, ear-ringing alliteration (Swinburne as a "libidinous laureate," etc.), which must have tickled Morley's peevish fancy, tends to obscure the intelligence and good sense with which he approached one of the most controversial poets of the past hundred years. Morley was no hidebound moralist as some would have it. In Swinburne's poetry he recognized idiosyncrasies that later critics, particularly in the twentieth century, would analyze with great relish. It is to his credit as a reader that he sensed certain psychological irregularities in the sexual evocation of Swinburne's lines, and it is even more to his credit as an honest critic and journalist that he had the nerve to discuss them publicly in print at a time when few would have admitted they even existed. In fact, he had no quarrel with Swinburne and was rather well disposed toward him generally. A similar example of Morley's insightful criticism is found in his review of Browning's *Ring and the Book* in 1869 where he had the foresight to argue that the book's virtue was where time has shown it most decidedly to be—in its style rather than its subject matter. At the time, most other contemporary critics were faulting the book for the obscurity of its subject matter.[5]

His method of literary criticism was also singular for the times, less conventionally didactic and impressionistic than most and, though he admired and was admittedly influenced by Arnold's approach to literature as a "criticism of life," much more historically centered. Like Arnold he desired to see the object as it really was and to discuss what it could or could not do for mankind, but he chose to concentrate his focus as well on where it belonged in the vast continuum of ideas and in the intellectual currents and historical forces that shaped an age. His method was synthetic. He argued in his essay on Byron that a great writer expresses a vision or philosophy of life, and that that is the test of his greatness. The critic, in turn, is obliged to synthesize the complements that constitute the great writer's genius, to reconstruct his mind, and then to relate it to the age. It was not enough for a critic to show *how* a work came to be written; he insisted that the critic must also demonstrate its truth; he must "trace the relations of the poet's ideas . . . through the central currents of thought, to the visible tendencies of an existing age."[6]

There is a definite sense of purpose in Morley's criticism that continues to make him readable and informative. But what gives him the authority and credibility that is not found in the work of many of his contemporaries is the self-confident integrity and daring that characterized his life, and that eventually set the tone for his works as well as for the journal that he

65

edited.[7] It was the same type of self-confidence that enabled him to give Pater a fair and intelligent reading when others were unable to find any enduring, substantive value at all in his essays.

Morley took over the editorship of the *Fortnightly Review* in 1867. The journal had been originally founded in 1865 by Anthony Trollope, Cotter Morison, and Frederic Chapman in order to give writers a forum for freedom of speech and opinion.[8] Each writer was to sign his articles, an unorthodox procedure for the period, since the most prominent periodicals still held to the traditional principle of keeping articles anonymous. No review with signed articles before the *Fortnightly* managed to survive. But then the *Fortnightly* was unlike any journal that had preceded it.

The first editor was George Henry Lewes and he established the policy that the magazine be dedicated to aiding progress and the cause of liberalism regardless of the direction it took, a policy that lasted through Morley's tenure. But the magazine under Lewes was a financial failure. In 1867 Lewes resigned and Morley who was but twenty-eight at the time took over. Morley retained the old open-ended editorial policy as much as possible, but it was inevitable, given the regular contributors to the journal (Mill, Bagehot, Huxley, Tyndall, Stephen), that it should become primarily the organ of liberalism. Under Morley's direction, the journal prospered. It was widely read and it remained controversial. One of his contributors wrote and told him that he would rather publish in the *Fortnightly* even though he could make more money by writing for other journals because things that appeared in the *Fortnightly* were "more talked about."[9] Just how controversial the journal was is pointed up by a story told by J. A. Spender in 1938. Spender recalled that in 1888 a staunchly evangelical relative of his with whom he was staying found a copy of Morley's *Fortnightly* in his bedroom. The over-zealous relative picked it up with a pair of tongs, carried it to the kitchen and placed it in the fire.[10] The story, F. W. Knickerbocker assures us, was not unusual. There are supposedly other accounts of the magazine being burned by some of the orthodox in protest over its liberal views. Some also wrote sharp protests to Morley, to which he replied that his primary motivation in printing the controversial essays—fully realizing that they were controversial (and probably relishing the fact)—was out of "respect for truth."[11]

Though Morley obviously welcomed the controversy (what editor concerned with the economics of publishing magazines would not?), he was honest in his response. For the *Fortnightly* was dedicated to "truth" in the pursuit of which it encouraged a free and open discussion of religious issues, a discussion of issues designed to popularize thinking—to bring the most heated issues to the man in the street—and, Morley hoped, to foster eventually a revolution in the intellectual habits of its readers that would in turn create a climate responsive to positive social action.[12] The first and most extensive controversy that the *Fortnightly* involved itself in was the battle against orthodoxy. It was fought in the pages of the journal by Spencer, Herschel, Stephen, Tyndall, Huxley, and, of course, Morley himself. More than just disenchantment with traditional theology, it was believed to be a battle for the freedom of individual intellectual thought, the liberty of the mind. Looking back on that challenge to orthodoxy, Morley in his *Recollections*, written in 1917, remembers Huxley and recalls that in his publications his object was, like Morley's own, "to promote the increase of natural knowledge." There could be no alleviation for the sufferings of mankind, Huxley argued; his call to action insisted on "veracity of thought and action, and the resolute facing of the world as it is, when the garment of make-believe, by which pious hands have hidden its uglier features, is stripped off."[13]

It was into this select circle of liberal thinkers that Pater was admitted by Morley in 1869 with the publication of the da Vinci essay. What Pater shared with the liberal phalanx of the *Fortnightly* was "liberalism" in the broad sense of the term, but it was also a brand of liberalism that Morley linked with his own preoccupation at the time with Positivism. The early influence of Positivism on Morley's thought is recalled in his *Recollections*. It is not hard to see, as well, the association that Positivist thinking had on his sense of the social mission of the *Fortnightly*. The English disciples of Comte were known to Morley through his association with Lewes and George Eliot, both of whom he viewed as staunch adherents of Comtean Positivism. George Eliot, he noted, had regularly assured him that she saw no reason why Comte's Religion of Humanity should not take root.[14] He also had great admiration for the Positivists as distinguished writers and unselfish and devoted workers for the social good. The result was that the entire system, but especially Comte's survey of history, laid a strong hold on him. It was, finally, his anti-sectarian instinct that kept him from uniting with them formally. And though official Positivism was viewed by those like Spencer, Tyndall, and Huxley rather suspiciously, as Catholicism minus Christianity, the idea of progress and the theory of history that formed much of its thought greatly appealed to him. So much so that he claimed that it was actually his involvement with Positivism that led him to absorb the lesson that became the golden rule of his life—"to do justice to truths presented and services rendered by men in various schools" even if he found himself in disagreement with them. This attraction to diverse modes of thought was part of what Morley viewed as the "triumph of the principle of relativity in historic judgment" in contrast to a servile and mind-limiting dependence on absolutes.[15]

The Positivist spirit, if not official Positivism, seems as well to have gripped Pater during those years. His early essays owed much to his reading of Mill, Huxley, Herbert Spencer, and John Tyndall, as well as to G. H. Lewes' work on Comte. And though, as Gerald Monsman recently pointed out, one cannot identify specific articles written by those who led the new wave of rationalism as definite sources for anything in particular that Pater wrote, nevertheless, his early writings drew imaginatively on the sciences (biology, chemistry, physics, and geology) for terminology, in an effort, it seems, to use the authority of science as the Positivists did to bolster his views on the progress of history.[16] But what distinguished Pater particularly in the eyes of Morley—and he appears to have been the only early critic to have seen it—was not so much Pater's grasp of Positivist scientific theory, which was noticeably limited, but his open support in those early essays for the more general spirit of scientism, liberal thinking, and the progressive opinions of leading rationalist thinkers of the time.

The first of Pater's essays that Morley accepted for publication was "Leonardo da Vinci" (November 1869). In it Morley must have been delighted to find a sustained, graphically presented defense of the modern scientific spirit. Here Pater argued for da Vinci's contribution in a new, uniquely modern critical fashion. He noted, for instance, that da Vinci's genius was to be found in two elementary forces: his curiosity and his desire for beauty. True, he sought to satisfy his great curiosity through a return to nature, but it was significantly "a microscopic sense" of nature's finish; an awareness of nature's role as a new source for scientific study which developed concurrently with the "modern spirit." The result was that da Vinci purposely sought out the company of men of science—for instance, "Fra Luca Paccioli the mathematician, and the anatomist Marc Antonio della Torre." Collected, da Vinci's manuscripts filled thirteen volumes and those who can judge described him as anticipating as early as the fifteenth century, "by rapid intuition, the later ideas of science." For example, "he explained the obscure light of the unilluminated part of the moon, knew that the sea had once covered the mountains which contain shells, and of the gathering of the equatorial waters above the polar." And thus, the argument continues, da Vinci reflected his scientific curiosity for the secret and remote aspects of nature in his paintings, landscapes of places far withdrawn. And it was with the same curiosity that he plunged into the subject of character; *La Gioconda*, for instance, the symbol of the "modern idea" that humanity sums up in itself, "all modes of thought and life." Pater also acknowledges at the end of the essay that mere "antiquarianism" should be of little importance in any true estimate of Leonardo's artistic genius. Antiquarian concerns over such matters as whether or not Francis the First was present at the time of his death, he urges, should be overshadowed by more valuable speculation about da Vinci's desire for beauty, his scientific interest in natural forms or his great curiosity.[17] Pater's criticism of those futile, antiquarian methods of study was probably what Morley had in mind later in his review of the *Renaissance* when he singled out for praise Pater's own attempt to redeem "beautiful production ... from the arid bondage of ... technicalities" and, especially, his praiseworthy ability, by contrast, to do the fullest justice to a subject on independent grounds.[18] And so there was much for Morley to applaud both in Pater's defense of the scientific spirit in the da Vinci essay and in his rendering of the essential qualities of da Vinci's artistic and scientific character. Morley must have been equally pleased with Pater's handling of character in the other essays that he published in the *Fortnightly*, for the analytical method was essentially the same. The sentiments they seem to have shared indicate a strong intellectual bond between them. Whether the influence was more direct than that is uncertain.

Edward Alexander, however, in his recent study of Morley, suggests that several of Pater's critical views may have been directly informed by Morley's thoughts on the relationship between literature and science; that Pater's 1867 essay on Winckelman, for instance, contained ideas that closely resembled ideas that Morley had developed earlier in his 1866 review of Victor Hugo. Alexander also suggests that they shared a common theory of tragedy, based essentially on their respective readings of

Victor Hugo, and that Pater, like Morley, argued for the Positivist idea that historical beliefs and theories were to be viewed relatively in terms of characteristics relative to a particular period in time.[19] Though Alexander's argument is appealing, the similarity between their thoughts was more likely the result of a kindred spiritual and intellectual relationship than of any direct influence.

Positivism had advanced the theory that all historical periods were interrelated. Questions of the superiority or inferiority of historical epochs were inapplicable, an idea that Pater echoed in the "Preface" to *The Renaissance* and elsewhere in his anti-Ruskinian defense of the fundamental equality of all ages and epochs. Historical events, according to this theory, were to be satisfactorily understood only through the knowledge of conditions relative to the time in which they occurred. Characteristics of historical epochs were not, therefore, to be criticized or evaluated apart from the additional knowledge of the conditions of the times. For an historical phenomenon that, in the present, might seem barbaric or primitive may well have fulfilled certain valuable needs at the time. Such cultural and historical phenomena, it follows, could only be fully understood and evaluated through the knowledge of the times and of the needs they fulfilled. In short, history was a science, to be studied as a science; though not necessarily with the kind of rigid erudition that a scholar such as Mark Pattison may have preferred. Morley saw that Pater, like himself, had recognized the new currents of scientific thought that had arisen in the nineteenth century and within which the "modern" artist would now have to function; in particular, Pater had a sense of history that in Morley's eyes was sympathetic with Positivist objectives. Certainly, his acceptance for publication of the early essays and his favorable, highly supportive review of *The Renaissance* were not based on the belief that Pater had totally embraced Positivism; but instead that Pater, like the Positivists, though for different ends, in the words of Alexander, "used the historical method to show that all institutions and beliefs were only 'right' and 'true' for their particular periods, not absolutely and eternally."[20]

The new currents of Positivist and scientific thought to which Morley addressed himself were mainly European and predominantly French in origin. Of course, the impact of Mill on his thought was always foremost: he called Mill his intellectual father and his career, in one sense, may be viewed as a lifelong effort to build on the theories of liberal utilitarianism that he initially learned from Mill. But next to Mill, the primary formative influences on his thought were French.

In his French studies and in many of his reviews, Morley tried to nudge English criticism, as Arnold earlier had done, away from stuffy parochialism and in the direction of the mainstream of much broader continental European thought. And though, like Arnold, he admired French intellectual achievement, he nevertheless deplored what he believed were French morals. On one occasion, he threw two works of French fiction out of the window in disgust while travelling from Paris to Calais.[21] But then intellectual achievement was the product of individual genius and not necessarily to be viewed as conjugate with a nation's morality or its fiction. Frederic Harrison, in response to one of Morley's vituperative criticisms of the French, wrote to him in 1872, "I am amused at your tirade against the poor French. Your literary spleen drives you into droll contradictions. . . . If what you say of the French is true your whole life has been a mistake. It has been devoted to popularizing the French social and political ideas. . . . What is it that is about to place you in the first rank of living writers—your *Voltaire*, your Voltairean estimate and conception of the most typical of Frenchmen. Why is your *Review* flowing over with French ideas, French history, and French systems?"[22] Of course, Harrison was correct. Especially during the 'seventies, Morley was immersed in French thought. In 1871 in the first edition of *Critical Miscellanies*, he published his studies of the Marquis de Vauvenargues, Antoine Nicolas Condorcet and Joseph de Maistre; the Condorcet and Vauvenargues had been published earlier in *Fortnightly* in 1870 (Condorcet in January and February; Vauvenargues in April); the essay on de Maistre in 1868 in *Fortnightly*. In 1872 he published the book length study of Voltaire that Harrison refers to; his study of Rousseau followed in two volumes in 1873. In 1876 in the August, September, and November issues of the *Fortnightly*, he published "Robespierre." *Diderot and the Encyclopaedists* appeared in two volumes in 1878 after more than three years of writing and research. The extent of his output was indeed considerable for a man who claimed to have disliked the French.

His French studies were designed to incorporate a type of implicit comparative analysis of the philosophical and religious traditions of thought of France and England, with a decided preference, of course, for eighteenth-century French thought. By doing so, he was challenging a strong element of negative criticism of the eighteenth century that existed during the Victorian era. Allowing for the hazards of over-extended analogies, it might well be compared to a similar wave of negativism that was spearheaded by Lytton Strachey and other disillusioned "moderns" who were bent on setting the world of their Victorian elders squarely on its ear shortly after the turn of the twentieth century. In the Victorian age, the eighteenth century remained for many a time of spiritual paralysis and infidelity. Morley placed much of the blame for the misinterpretation at the feet of Carlyle who had impressed upon his generation, according to Morley, a damaging one-sided view of the eighteenth century and of eighteenth-century French thinkers particularly.[23] Gosse, in 1919, in "The Agony of the Victorian Age," recalled that it was particularly the great influence of French thought in the eighteenth century that first was objected to and then, he adds, eventually completely denied by the Victorians. Morley took up the challenge created by that denial in the 1870's, admitting to the influence of Comte on his decision, and attempted to revive interest not only in the eighteenth century but in eighteenth-century French thought as well. One must assume that in his effort, he welcomed all of the help he could get. He did encounter some opposition. His political opponents later in the 'eighties used his French studies to discredit him (the anti-French sentiment was still that strong), an attempt that he responded to in 1888 in "A Few Words on French Models," in which he accused his attackers of having calcined blood and of naively entertaining demons.[24] His French studies were viewed as a defense of Jacobinism and he was reproached for being a revolutionary. But Morley envisioned himself as less a revolutionary than a spokesman entrusted with rescuing the great writers of the French Enlightenment and enlisting them in the cause of liberalism in nineteenth-century England. The choice of his subject matter, however, remained for the time, inflammatory. Even late nineteenth-century Englishmen were still suspicious of writers who devoted too much of their literary energy to French sources. The days of resentment and outrage directed at yellow-backed volumes from France had not yet passed; and one recalls, though it occurred earlier, Jane Eyre's uncharitable observation in Charlotte Bronte's novel, that Adele, Rochester's ward, prattled and displayed a superficiality of character that was probably inherited from her French mother and that was "hardly congenial to an English mind."[25] Voltaire was still viewed as an infidel; Rousseau was destructive. Neither had a very serious place in Britain's post-Romantic intellectual thought; and the pattern was equally repressive for most of the other great intellectuals associated with the French Enlightenment.

And so Morley recognized in Pater an ally, not only owing to his leanings toward Positivism but also, and more generally, to the overall intellectual tradition which he seemed to represent, one that was rooted squarely in the center of liberal, European thought, with a distinctly eighteenth-century slant. Indeed, many of Pater's personal preferences and tastes seem to have been decidedly European, even to his preference in scenery. He wrote to William Sharp in 1882, "at the end of this month [November] I hope to leave for seven weeks in Italy, chiefly at Rome, where I have never yet been. We went to Cornwall for our summer holiday, but though that country is certainly very singular and beautiful, I found there not a tithe of the stimulus to one's imagination which I have sometimes experienced in quite unrenowned places abroad."[26] The promise of the south and sunnier climates? Perhaps, but one should also remember that even in his taste for architecture, Pater seems to have had a distinct preference for French cathedrals—and northern ones at that.[27]

Pater's leanings toward European taste and thought are displayed with regular frequency in his writings. In *The Renaissance*, for instance, there are extensive references to European intellectuals—artists, particularly: Charles Sainte-Beuve, Jean Cousin, Germain Pilon, Victor Hugo, Jules Michelet, Bernard de Ventadour, Pierre Vidal, Heinrich Heine, Marsilio Ficino, as well as Goethe, Hegel, Comte, Dante, and writers of the French Enlightenment such as Voltaire and Rousseau. All are treated as familiar figures in a pantheon of artists and intellectuals; all attest to his interest in European thought and also to the eclectic nature of his reading. His deep interest in the Renaissance itself is rooted in the Renaissance as he envisioned it developing particularly on the European continent, especially in France and Italy. Of the former, he writes, that it was the French Renaissance that put forth the "wonderful later growth" whose products realize to the fullest the subtle and delicate sweetness that he associated with the Renaissance spirit. Of Italy, he writes that it was precisely there in the fifteenth century that the full interest of the Renaissance is to be found, "in that solemn fifteenth century which can hardly be studied too much, not merely for its positive results in the things of the intellect and the imagination, its concrete works of art, its special and prominent per-

sonalities . . . but for its general spirit and character, for the ethical qualities of which it is a consummate type."[28] Pater's leanings toward European
taste and thought also accounted in some measure for Morley's interest in
him; they worshipped at the same altars. And though the catalog of European intellectuals who appealed to them individually during those years
does vary somewhat, as one would expect, there was no variance at all in
the mutual admiration they both had for Victor Hugo, an admiration
that accounts for another important link between them.

In 1874, the year after his review of Pater appeared, Morley wrote
an essay on "Victor Hugo's 'Ninety-Three.' "[29] It was his second essay
devoted to Hugo. His first was a review of *Toilers of the Sea* that was
published, unsigned, in *Saturday Review* for April 7, 1866. The 1866
review reflected Morley's deep emotional response to Hugo's treatment
of nature, specifically his treatment of the sea's mighty power and its capa-
city for destruction, which Morley believed was an awareness fundamental
to Hugo's tragic vision. The same tragic vision with its emphasis on the
immensity and power of nature, is referred to again by Morley in his
review of *Ninety-Three*, in Hugo's dark, brooding descriptions of the
forests of La Vendée. If the waves in *Toilers of the Sea*, he writes, are
appalling in their thunderous power, the forest in *Ninety-Three* is appalling in its silence, its great mystery, and in the invisibility of the many
thousands of forms of life for which it provides shelter.[30] For Morley,
Hugo treats the idea of tragedy by instinct and circumstance, not design;
and it is his depth of tone that makes him singular. To analyze Hugo's
concept of the tragic is to probe "the very heart of science," for tragedy
to Hugo, as Morley envisioned it, is "a thing of cause and effect, invariable
antecedent and invariable consequent." Consequently, no living writer,
Morley adds, is so "consummate a master of landscape."[31]

Pater also was attracted to Victor Hugo's enlightened, instinctively
scientific response to nature, particularly landscape, and as well to the
romantic tone that it created. In "The Poetry of Michelangelo," first published by Morley in the *Fortnightly* in 1871, which Morley read approv-
ingly, Pater writes that what is primarily important about men of inven-
tive temper like Michelangelo and Hugo (he might have added da Vinci,
as well) is that they enhance and lighten erudite conceptions of the
spiritual through the treatment of real phenomena, or what he calls
"accessories"; but, he adds, that though Michelangelo employs accessories,

he is too austere to focus on accessories drawn from the world of physical nature in the scientific fashion of Victor Hugo. Better if he had, for Hugo accomplishes more. He gives special attention to the natural phenomena of life, "like the butterfly which alights on the blood-stained barricade in *Les Misérables*," or the "sea-birds for whom the monstrous Gilliatt comes to be as some wild natural thing . . . in *Les Travailleurs de la Mer*."[32] Morley, in 1866, while reviewing the same novel for *Saturday Review*, had made the same point—that the strength of the novel came from Hugo's scientific treatment of physical nature as something even far more important and expressive than the world of man. But Morley extended his interpretation a bit farther than Pater to include the claim that Hugo was expressing in his art the Positivist notion that the natural world is not subject to laws prescribed by gods or men; dogmatic pronouncements had their limitations, and all one had to do to realize that fact was to look scientifically to the colossal power and seemingly endless potential for destruction that is found in physical nature. By comparison, man and his abstract dogmas appeared pitiful and frail.

Pater and Morley also shared the idea that Hugo's was a voice set against religious absolutism. In *The Renaissance*, Pater notes that one of the strongest characteristics of the outbreak of scientific reason and imagination which partially characterized the Renaissance spirit for him was its "antinomianism, its spirit of rebellion and revolt against the moral and religious ideas of the time." It was also found in the search for the pleasures of the senses and imagination, the care for physical beauty, the worship of the body. And, he adds, it is "this rebellious and antinomian element" that has made the delineation of the Middle Ages by Victor Hugo and other writers of the Romantic school in France so appealing.[33]

Later, writing in *Recollections*, Morley acknowledged having been, as a young man, completely overtaken by Hugo. He writes of revelling in his books, of being "stirred to the depths . . . by the noble, tender, elevated, and pitying moral pulse that beat in his verse or prose."[34] Though not nearly as overwhelmed by Hugo, Pater does argue in his conclusion to the "Michelangelo" essay that perhaps the chief use that comes from continuing the study of Michelangelo is that the virtues of sweetness and strength that recommend him are to be found more frequently in contemporary writers than in his own followers; and that among the more contemporary writers embodying those virtues, Blake and Hugo, in particular, are Michelangelo's true sons, helping us to understand him as he in turn helps us to understand them.[35] It is also particularly significant that the last paragraph of the "Conclusion," the final essay in *The Renaissance*, and the essay that calls openly for a life of quickened, multiplied experiences in the love of "art for art's sake," is structured on two basic references, one drawn from Rousseau and the other from Victor Hugo. Of Rousseau, Pater writes that one of the most beautiful passages in *Confessions* is in the sixth book where he describes his awakening to the literary sense. Fearing for his life, Rousseau asked himself how he might make the most of the time that was left to him before he should die. His decision was that it would be in the pursuit of the kind of intellectual excitement that he had found in his reading of Voltaire. A similar recognition of the mortal paradox, the sentence of death, and the need to make the most of the natural time alloted to us, Pater continues, is to be found as well in the works of Hugo. We have the interval and then we are no more; the wisest of us, " 'the children of the world,' " spend that interval in art and song.[36] Rousseau and Hugo, with Voltaire in the background, all revolutionary defenders of the natural sciences, stand significantly at the end of this most important statement of Pater's vision of how one truly lives the "aesthetic" life. Morley must have been delighted: Rousseau and Hugo were enshrined as exemplars of intellectual excitement pointing the scientific and natural direction that discriminating, free-thinking tastes must follow. Though Pater's interest in Hugo and what he represented does not extend to the limits that Morely envisioned, nevertheless, he did have a high place reserved for Hugo in his gallery of European scientific thinkers. It is another instance of that affinity in spirit and intellect that Pater seems to have shared with Morley. On that score, it is not hard to understand why he was so enthusiastically taken with the essays of the young Oxford scholar.

Morley was also preoccupied with concepts of good character; he believed that one of the great benefits of reading literature was that it had the potential for elevating character and, consequently, elevating the whole of mankind. His interest in character led naturally, as Warren Staebler suggests, to an enthusiastic study of the lives of great men, even mutually antagonistic great men such as Cromwell and Burke or Rousseau and Voltaire.[37] Each great life manifested in itself elements which, when isolated and viewed individually, benefited civilization. The key to critical studies of great men, Morley advised, was to find the elements that recommended or that distinguished that particular figure of greatness. Significantly, it is similar to what Pater in the "Preface" to *The Renaissance* advocated as the primary objective of the aesthetic critic—that is, the need to isolate the "virtue," the strength of the work or the character.

Morley's interest in the great man is reflected particularly in his portraits of great French intellects like Diderot and Voltaire who had a passion for social action and who attempted to alter, through the power of the intellect, the course of human history. The artistic and literary heroes depicted in Pater's *Renaissance*, on the other hand, were not directly responsible for altering the course of human history, but they were instrumental, as Pater envisioned them, in creating an intellectual climate out of which those major social alterations would develop. It is particularly significant that Morley recognized as well that the ability to create an intellectual climate conducive to change was also a central, intrinsic characteristic of Pater's own contemporary efforts in the portraits. He observed that "one of the first among the many fertilising agents" that the present time demands is exactly the kind of "sincere and disinterested work . . . upon exactly such subjects as Mr. Pater has chosen, real yet detached from the clamour of to-day."[38] Pater's treatment of the theme of the great man, in this case, specifically, the great artist and man of letters, and his own efforts to create a climate of change recommended the essays collected in *The Renaissance* to Morley as much as the support of scientism, Positivism, and other decidedly liberal and advanced currents of European thought that Morley found there as well.

The strengths of *The Renaissance* were solid and ample enough for him to overlook other, less appealing aspects. And he did find elements in the book to which he objected. When it came out in 1873 he explained to Frederic Harrison, his close friend, "I think it very desirable to call attention to any book like Pater's, which is likely to quicken public interest in the higher sorts of literature. And, moreover, a young and unknown writer like him ought to be formally introduced to the company by the hired master of ceremonies, myself, or another to wit. So pray pardon my light dealing with his transgressions."[39] Just what the "transgressions" were that he had in mind is not clear unless he meant a certain tinge of obscurity that he noticed, especially in the "Winckelmann" essay which had been originally published in 1867 in the rival *Westminster Review*;

or, perhaps, he had in mind Pater's defense of the doctrine of "art for art's sake" which he judged an incomplete scheme for either wise living or wise dying. Yet, he argued, certainly to the shock and amazement of Pater's enemies, that, in spite of a limited deficiency in wisdom, the doctrine of "art for art's sake," regardless of what its detractors claimed, was no impediment to positive social change; in fact, it fostered an attitude that attempted to bring what he called "the aesthetical element" around to the common concerns of daily life. It was an idea that he thought should be supported for it was, like the Oxford movement out of which he believed it grew, "equally a protest against the mechanical and graceless formalism of the modern era, equally an attempt to find a substitute for a narrow popular creed in a return upon the older manifestations of the human spirit, and equally a craving for the infusion of something harmonious and beautiful about the bare lines of daily living."[40] Oxford's Newmanite generation, he adds, had been followed in England by the revolutionary generation of which Pater now was a representative, a generation that was formed largely by Mill and Grote's history of Greece. It was also a generation that he believed would drive needed wedges at crucial points into the block of English philistinism.[41] One wonders how less enthusiastic critics of Pater's *Renaissance* such as Mrs. Oliphant, W. H. Mallock or W. J. Stillman might have responded to Morley's argument. Unfortunately, there are no records or accounts. But Morley had provided a defense that would have answered some of the charges and claims of unsound reasoning and historical inaccuracy that they had raised against Pater.

Morley's review of *The Renaissance* is an excellent example of his self-styled synthetic criticism. He sets out to accomplish two basic objectives: first, he relates the book to a great movement of liberal, scientific thought; and, second, he attempts to explain the value of the book for its time. Addressing the second concern, he notes that there was developing at the time a new, learned school of criticism, a hopeful sign for those concerned with the intellectual energy of the country and a corrective for a type of parochialism that he believed was stifling British thought, particularly British literary thought. His complaint was that too little attention was being given in England to the mainstream of European ideas: Tennyson is judged provincial, "too blind to the new forces"; and Browning is too metaphysical and obscure. Consequently, Morley claimed there were no literary leaders in England who worked in the central current of European thought. At least the early years of the century, he argued, had "a Scottish romance-writer" and a decidedly "inferior" poet who made the effort. The first reference, of course, is to Scott. The second seems to have been to Byron who was inferior but only as a poet in Morley's judgment. But Byron's "inferiority" diminished when held up against his major strength, the subordination of his poetic inclination to his social, political, and revolutionary intentions, all of which, in fact, made him distinctly "superior" in Morley's eyes.[43] But at present in England, Morley argued, far too many critical literary efforts are decidedly insular and trivial, a waste of time. And so, what was needed, he claimed, was nothing less than a distinct opening of new channels to the continent. But the tide, he added, was shifting. For there were a few young British writers of active spirit, "as yet unknown beyond limited circles, and still wavering in intellectual direction," from which there was good reason to expect a literature that would again open the channels, that would unite, for instance, "German excellence of research and power of historic vision with French excellence of presentation and skill in grouping."[44] Criticism of the highest kind, he predicted, would be the natural forerunner of this new literary movement and also would be the earliest form that the movement would take. He advised the critic who wished to associate himself with the new wave to first detach himself from the hubbub made by the "rival partisans in philosophy and philosophical theology," an effort that naturally should take the form of criticism of the past which, for Morley, was the only advisable way to impart ideas while yet remaining aloof and free from present agitations. The criticism of the three or four young writers that he had in mind, he added, is genuine and largely so, because, alluding to Arnold, it is wholly "disinterested." They use their doctrines as instruments and their subjects as illustrations, but they also do complete justice to the subject on independent grounds. Significantly, it is the independent treatment that is also their primary aim. Thus, he added, finally linking the new school of criticism directly with his own Positivist interests, "they help to create a literary atmosphere which is not choked with the acrid fumes of battle, they spread a disposition for *positive* thought."[45]

Of course, Pater was one of this select group of young writers because he emphasized the need for open, independent evaluation, and because he was also a supporter of the theory that advanced the need to emphasize relative judgments in all things. In *On Compromise*, published in 1903, Morley argued that "the marked progress of criticism and interpretation of life has been the substitution of becoming for being, the relative for the absolute, dynamic movement for dogmatic immobility."[46] Thirty years before, Morley had envisioned the essays in *The Renaissance* as remarkable examples of this fresh critical approach to life and to art. Pater was not only a relativist, he argued, but also a master stylist: coherent yet subtle; his thought is ordered; his intellectual firmness usually keeps the tendency to eloquence in his style under control. But primarily his criticism is "concrete and *positive*, not metaphysical; a record of impressions, not an analysis of their ultimate composition, nor an abstract search for the law of their effects."[47] It is to Pater's credit, he adds, that he betrays an impatience with abstraction. What is important, in Pater's words, "is not that the critic should possess a correct abstract definition of beauty, but a certain kind of temperament, the power of being deeply moved by the presence of beautiful objects." He also quotes Pater on the need for this new positive thinking critic to disengage the particular quality that distinguishes the beautiful object from commoner elements, to disengage it and mark it. This keen, scientific attraction, he continues, to the minute, to the particular, underlies his love for the "faintly marked traces of exquisite peculiarity, rather than the noon-day splendor of master works." Gregorian chant would probably please him more than a Beethoven symphony; for, after all, he adds, "anybody may be stirred by the sublime or the superb."[48]

It is also to Pater's credit, Morley argues, that he insists on associating art with the real moods and purposes of mankind. He has a distinct, concrete theory of life that involves living with quickened senses, of seeking through art or "art for art's sake" to add only the highest quality to a life style, to "moments" that are not restricted or limited only to privileged celebrated occasions, but that can be appreciated in common daily life as well. Before the appearance of Pater and the other critics of this new school, Morley adds, "there never was seen . . . in this country so distinct an attempt to bring the aesthetical element closely and vividly round daily life." It is this effort at some kind of intellectual expansion into the daily lives of people that must precipitate social change, the object again of Positivist action.[49]

That Pater attempted to bring the merits of art down to the world of daily existence and to show the spectator or the reader, whoever or wherever he might be, how to savor the pleasure independently, on his own terms, without absolute pronouncements or the instructive prescription of the specialists, is Morley's most permanently valuable critical observation on Pater's intellectual contribution to the democratization of art. In an address in 1887 to the students of the London Society for the Extension of University Teaching on the then controversial subject of the study and teaching of English literature, Morley called their attention to the great need to bring literature and the other arts to the people, to the common man. "Our object is," he told the students, "—and it is that which ... raises us infinitely above the Athenian level—to bring the Periclean ideas of beauty and simplicity and cultivation of the mind within the reach of those who do the drudgery and the service and rude work of the world. . . . And it can be done without blunting or numbing the practical energies of our people."[50] Morley was addressing himself to a timeless and particularly important objective of students and teachers of literature; and it is much to his credit as a critic that he realized that it was an objective to which Pater had also made an important contribution. But Morley was the only critic at the time who seems to have recognized that particular virtue in Pater's work.

Surely, Morley's primary strength as a critic was his incisive, penetrating honesty. Whether he was dealing with Voltaire or Burke or, on a more limited scale, with Pater, there are no heavy fogs or oily puddles in his criticism. It is hard to understand why he has been denied his place in the literary critical canon. He had his weaknesses as a critic, but they were never so great as to overshadow his honesty and his conspicuous courage. He consistently said new things and offered provocative insights—even when he was wrong. And he was wrong, remarkably wrong, especially about Yeats and other "moderns" who after the turn of the century, left him with a nagging and threatening presentiment that it was no longer his world that he was reading about.[51] His world, to the end of his life, seems to have been the Victorian world. But he should not be faulted for that. His judgments on the Victorian world and Victorian letters, since he saw them both in a way most Victorian literary critics could not, should be attended to as serious and instructive commentaries on the times. For who should be more knowledgeable about the Victorians and their world than a self-proclaimed Victorian himself?

Morley's greatest weakness as a critic seems to have been his enthusiasm; that is, his tendency to overstate, to over-extend his analyses at times. But in his defense, one might add that, at least, he always made the effort in his analyses to deal in substance rather than vapor. His tendency to over-state was a flaw that in his honesty he recognized himself and readily admitted. In 1888, in "A Few Words on French Models," looking in retrospect on the 'seventies, during which he wrote most of his French studies as well as his review of Pater, he admitted that he may have been "too eager" and the fault was reflected in the tone of some of the works; but, he added, that "to be eager is not a very bad vice at any age under the critical forty."[52] One might add, in addition, that there is little that he produced, even if, in his eagerness, it came out a bit lopsided, that is not compensated for a hundredfold by what he does say that is perceptive and thought-provoking, whether we agree or not.

In the case of Pater in particular, he does seem to have been on the mark most of the time. Where he falls short is in his insistence on weighing the Positivist elements more heavily than other elements that also con-tributed to the totality of Pater's vision, for instance, his interest in Hegel and Renaissance Humanism. Morley also exaggerates the extent of anti-religious sentiment in *The Renaissance*, insisting at times that the book is a sustained and intentional attack on Christianity, in which Pater raises aestheticism "to the throne lately filled by religion," an effort that Morley, in his "eagerness," adds is a perfect demonstration of Pater's success in showing "how void the old theologies have become."[53] Ironically, given his difficulties at Oxford after the appearance of *The Renaissance*, Pater would have been better off at the time without Morley's "high praise" of his anti-religious sentiment. But Morley intended for his readers to see a link between what he claimed was Pater's criticism of religion and his argument for the aesthetic life style as a more rational, democratic, and intellectual alternative. Unfortunately for Pater's reputation, particularly at Oxford, too many did see the link—and much too clearly. Finally, owing to the critical pressure, Pater removed the offending "Conclusion" in which he explained how one lives aesthetically, from the second edition of *The Renaissance* when it was published in 1877. Morley's review may not have had any direct affect on that move, but it certainly added fuel to a situation that was already inflammatory and threatening.

Basil Willey suggests that Morley was far more interested in the extra-literary than he was in the actual literary merits of a work; that he was chiefly interested in writers, for instance, when they clearly represented or had a place in some great movement in the onward march of history.[54] If Morley thought a writer worth the effort, he set out in his criticism to mark off a place for him in the great continuum of literary and historical thought. His estimation of Pater must have been high; at least, he thought he was worth the effort, because he attempted to establish a place for Pater's works as something other than "mere literature." He insisted on viewing him as an anti-orthodox defender of liberalism and the theories of Positivism. It is not exaggerating to say that he used Pater and *The Renaissance* to promote his own and the *Fortnightly*'s campaign for Positivism, but a Positivism that was certainly far more at home with the cause of liberalism in England than with Comte and France. To claim that Morley used Pater is not intended as a condemnation of his motives or a negative judgment of his character. By using some of Pater's ideas to support his ends, Morley was simply demonstrating his awareness of certain political and social facts of life; Morley was an astute politician and always a dedicated liberal reformer. Pater was a young unknown writer in the late 'sixties and early 'seventies, who needed an audience for his works. Morley offered him the pages of the *Fortnightly*. And though he did to some extent exaggerate and overstate Pater's position on certain points in his review, he never seems to have received any objections on that score from Pater, in spite of the effect the review must have had on those already incensed over his questionable religious and aesthetic pronouncements. But Pater was grateful for the help; the review was favorable and it attempted to make a case for his contribution that involved more than praise for his care of the paragraph or for his rhetorical mining in the subterranean depths of a literary shadow world. And that is greatly to Morley's credit.

His review of *The Renaissance*, with its trenchant and provocative observations on Pater, was nothing short of remarkable for 1873. Pater's detractors had found little to praise in his book; the supportive criticism, though well-intended, had provided little that was substantive. Only Morley, among his contemporaries, made an effort to see him in a broader and more scientific context. When the second edition of *The Renaissance* came out in 1877, Pater had a "blurb" from Morley's 1873 review included in the advertisements. The review may not have been totally on the mark, but Pater was grateful for the effort he had made. In a letter written to him shortly after the review appeared, Pater thanked him formally for attempting to explain his "ethical point of view," adding the rather curious and ambiguous remark, "to which I fancy some readers have given a prominence I did not mean it to have."[55]

Whether Morley himself should be included among those who gave the book a prominence Pater had not intended depends on how seriously one takes Morley's criticism. It is unfortunate, whether one agrees or not with his assessment of Pater, that more critics did not learn from his accounting of Pater's intellectual strengths during those early years. But few, even of Pater's later supporters, seem to have taken Morley's claims seriously. If they had, perhaps there might have been other accounts that would now prove as useful to students of the age. It was not until the 'nineties, at least, that Pater's reputation as a professional critic and man of letters began to assume anything like the far-reaching, intellectual dimensions that Morley prophetically had attempted to give it in the 'seventies.

NOTES

FOREWORD

[1] The essay was reprinted in 1933 in Saintsbury's *Prefaces and Essays* (London: Macmillan), esp., pp. 345-355. Subsequent textual references are to this edition.

[2] Harold Bloom, "Late Victorian Poetry and Pater," *Yeats* (New York: Oxford University Press, 1970), pp. 23-37.

CHAPTER I: EARLY DIRECTIONS

[1] A. C. Benson, *Walter Pater* (London: Macmillan, 1906); rptd. (Detroit: Gale Research, 1968), p. 174.

[2] Benson, p. 175.

[3] See *Letters of Walter Pater*, ed. Lawrence Evans (Oxford: Clarendon Press, 1970), p. 13.

[4] For the most thorough account to date of the reputation that Pater had acquired at Oxford during his years as a student and young lecturer, see Gerald Monsman, *Walter Pater* (Boston: G. K. Hall, 1977), pp. 26-33 and 62-65. Monsman writes that "Pater's brand of 'Germanism,'" during those early years "was so extreme that it was considered to be more akin to atheism than theology. S. R. Brooke, a conservative ... , described Pater's essay [given before the Old Mortality Society] as one of 'the most thoroughly infidel productions' to which it had ever been his 'pain' to listen" (pp. 29-30). On the reception of *The Renaissance* at Oxford, he notes that Oxford's "hothouse world" seems to have been far more outraged than the outside world; at Oxford it was treated like some heretical Christian treatise (pp. 63-64).

[5] See *Letters*, p. 14; "On one practical point perhaps you will allow me to ask a favour. Would you object to give up to myself or to the other tutors ... your share in the Divinity Examination in Collections? This is probably the last time in which the old system will be in force, and it would be, I confess, a relief to my mind if you would consent to do so" (p. 14).

[6] See Monsman, p. 64.

[7] Logan Piersall Smith, *Unforgotten Years* (London: Constable, 1938); rptd. (Boston: Little, Brown, 1939), pp. 191-194, 293.

[8] [Anonymous], "Pater's Studies of the Renaissance," *Saturday Review*, XXXVI (26 July 1873), 123-124; the reviewer notes that *The Renaissance* is also diametrically opposed to Ruskin's "famous dogma propounded in the Edinburgh Lectures"; yet he insists on making Pater out to be a disciple of Ruskin, equally prone to emotional epithets (p. 123).

[9] "New Books," *Blackwood's Edinburgh Magazine* (April 1871), pp. 440-441.

[10] [Margaret Oliphant], "New Books. XIV. Pater's History of the Renaissance," *Blackwood's Edinburgh Magazine* (November 1873), pp. 604-609.

[11] *The Autobiography and Letters of Mrs. M. O. W. Oliphant*, ed. by Mrs. Harry Coghill (Edinburgh and London: Blackwood and Sons, 1899), p. 4.

[12] *Ibid.*, pp. 115-116.

[13] *Ibid.*, pp. 3-4, 5.

[14] *Ibid.*, p. 5.

[15] *Ibid.*, p. 237.

[16] *Ibid.*, pp. 202-203

[17] *Ibid.*, p. 137.

[18] Vineta and Robert Colby, *Equivocal Virtue: Mrs. Oliphant and the Victorian Literary Marketplace* (Hamden, Conn.: Archon, 1966), pp. 189, 198; see also "The Sisters Bronte," in *Woman Novelists of Queen Victoria's Reign* (London: Hurst and Blackett, 1897); and "The Old Saloon," *Blackwood's Edinburgh Magazine* (March 1892), pp. 464-465. Writing on "The Royal Academy" in *Blackwood's* (June 1876), Mrs. Oliphant singles out the Pre-Ralphaelite lack of moderation for criticism, particularly John Everett Millais' "vulgar splendour" and Holman Hunt's "elaborate and far-fetched composition, trifling, and tedious from over-care, and those choice and recondite marvels of art which Mr. Rossetti and his school show to the initiated in the half-light of their studios, scorning the homely day and the common light" which we can be certain she would have preferred (p. 757).

[19] *The Bookman* (August 1897), p. 113.

[20] *The George Eliot Letters*, ed. Gordon S. Haight (New Haven: Yale University Press, 1954-1955), VI, 406.

[21] Henry James Nicoll, *Landmarks of English Literature* (New York: Appleton, 1883); rptd. (1888), pp. 440-441.

[22] Mrs. Oliphant's review of *Appreciations* appeared in "The Old Saloon. XXI," *Blackwood's Edinburgh Magazine* (January 1890), pp. 131-151, see especially pp. 140-145. Grant Allen (1848-1899) was a minor realistic novelist of the period. His most famous book was *The Woman Who Did*, published in 1895, after Mrs. Oliphant's review of *Appreciations*. Nevertheless, what he had published up to 1890, and it was considerable, impressed her. Harold Williams in 1918 wrote of Allen that though he was a

close student of character, his primary strength as a novelist, the necessity to earn a living drove him to write novels dictated by the taste of library subscribers. He wrote, as Mrs. Oliphant suggests, by necessity—to earn his oatmeal—not choice; and that is what Williams believes is fundamentally the problem with his works. In fifteen years, for instance, he wrote over thirty novels. He was a hard worker, but even the best of his novels, in Williams' opinion, had little permanent value. *The Woman Who Did* was hopelessly didactic; "the keen but deplorably narrow vision of the author, his inability to see far on either hand, and his burning desire scientifically to cleanse a smirched and soiled world, constantly intrude themselves upon the character-painting"; see Williams, *Modern English Writers*, Vol. II (1918); rptd. (Port Washington, N.Y.: Kennikat Press, 1970), 337-338. It is not difficult to see precisely why Mrs. Oliphant ranked him higher than Pater.

[23] W. H. Mallock, *The New Republic: Culture, Faith and Philosophy in an English Country House*, introd. by John Lucas (Leicester: Leicester University Press, 1975), p. 15.

[24] W. H. Mallock, *Memoirs of Life and Literature* (New York and London: Harper, 1920), pp. 364-365, 83; Mallock's consistent distaste for radicalism led him in 1889 in *Quarterly Review*, while reviewing John Morley's collected works, to call Morley "immoral" because of his liberalism and to brand him as "the Cardinal Newman of the Radical Movement." Morley must have been flattered by the comparison.

[25] See *The New Republic*, pp. 56, 232. Mallock believed that all of the mischief unleashed by "advanced" thought could only be undone by "a rational development of conservative thought" and by a revival of the "true faiths" upon which "the sanctities, the stabilities, and the civilization of the social order depend" (see his *Memoirs*, pp. 364-365).

[26] See *The New Republic*, p. 197.

[27] W. H. Mallock, *Aristocracy and Evolution* (New York and London: Macmillan, 1898), pp. 80-81.

[28] W. H. Mallock, *Property and Progress* (New York: Putnam's, 1884), pp. 162-164.

[29] *Memoirs of Life and Literature*, p. 277.

[30] *Ibid.*, pp. 364-365, 168.

[31] *The New Republic*, pp. 188-189.

[32] *Ibid.*, pp. 192-193.

[33] *Ibid.*, pp. 260, 262-263.

[34] "Preface," *The Renaissance* (London: Macmillan, 1910), p. xx.

[35] *Memoirs of Life and Literature*, pp. 79, 85.

[36] See Kenneth Clark, *Ruskin at Oxford* (Oxford: Clarendon Press, 1947), p. 4.

[37] See Geoffrey Tillotson, "Pater, Mr. Rose, and the 'Conclusion' of *The Renaissance*," in *Essays and Studies by Members of the English Association*, XXXII (1946); rptd. in *Criticism and the Nineteenth Century* (London: Athlone Press, 1951); rptd. (Hamden, Conn.: Archon, 1967), pp. 124-146.

[38] "Pater, Mr. Rose, and the 'Conclusion' of *The Renaissance*," pp. 124-146. Tillotson insists that Mallock's claim was disingenuous.

[39] Edmund Gosse, "Walter Pater: A Portrait," in *Critical Kit-Kats* (New York: Dodd, Mead and Co., 1896), pp. 257-258. Gosse writes that Pater was "flattered, for he was an author much younger and more obscure than most of those who were satirised, and he was sensible that to be thus distinguished was a compliment." What did really ruffle him, Gosse adds, "was the persistence with which the newspapers at this time began to attribute to him all sorts of 'aesthetic' follies and extravagances."

[40] Stillman knew Rossetti and J. M. W. Turner and had a long friendship with Ruskin, dating from the late 'forties. He was a successful art critic for the New York *Evening Post* and, later, worked as a special correspondent for the London *Times*. In 1855 he founded *Crayon: A Journal Devoted to the Graphic Arts, and the Literature Related to Them*. Through the journal, he formed valuable literary acquaintances, particularly from New England. In the late 'sixties, he settled in London. In 1898, he retired and moved to Surrey, where he died in 1901.

The great impact of Ruskin on Stillman's life is illustrated by the distinct possibility that his "native artistic bent" ran somewhat counter to Ruskin's tastes in art and eventually led him to make the crucial decision to abandon painting altogether around 1860 for a career in literature. But it is also likely that his understanding of artistic theory was far more advanced than his skill as a craftsman. He was interested in history and archaelogy; among his publications with historical interest are *The Acropolis of Athens* (1870); *The Old Rome and the New and Other Studies* (1898); and his works on Crete and Italy. His *Autobiography* was published in two volumes in 1901 (*DAB*).

[41] W. J. Stillman, "The Renaissance," *Nation* [NY], XVII (9 October 1873), 243-244.

[42] Sir Charles Dilke, her second husband, on the subject of her relationship to Ruskin, writes that "the influence which, earlier than that of Mark Pattison, was impressed upon her, was Ruskin's; but from Ruskin, deeply influenced as she was by him, she differed at every point." Ruskin wrote to her in 1887, "To obey me is to love Turner and hate Raphael, to love Goethe and hate Renaissance." But in spite of Ruskin's ultimatum, she seems not to have envisioned any real need to obey him. See Dilke's "Memoir" in *The Book of the Spiritual Life*, by the late Lady Dilke (London: John Murray; New York: Dutton, 1905); rptd. (New York: AMS Press, 1973), p. 28.

[43] See "Memoir," *The Book of the Spiritual Life*, p. 31; for additional information on her years at Oxford as Pattison's wife, see Kingsbury Badger, "Mark Pattison and the Victorian Scholar," *Modern Language Quarterly*,

VI (December 1945), 423-427. Badger provides particulars about Mrs. Pattison's life at Oxford and of the friendship between Mark Pattison and Pater; he also recalls Pater's remark to Gosse, after a visit to Pattison, that what Pattison apparently liked best was "romping with great girls in the gooseberry bushes."

44 Mrs. Mark Pattison, "Contemporary Literature. Art," *Westminster Review*, XLIII (April 1873), 639-640.

45 "Contemporary Literature. Art," p. 640.

46 See Pater's letter to Gosse, 10 September 1877, in *Letters of Walter Pater*, pp. 38-39; Pater writes to Gosse of having visited "Azay-le-Rideau, the most perfect of all those Loire Châteaux, concerning which Mrs. Mark Pattison seems, if I may judge from a rather rapid glance only at present, to have been writing well."

47 See "Memoir," *The Book of the Spiritual Life*, p. 28. Dilke writes of the rigors of his wife's scholarship, that she had "two sides to her intellectual life, and three diverse kinds of friends.... The 'Benedictine,' working always and everywhere, was understood by a few men in England and by a larger art-world abroad. One of these Englishmen writes to me, 'Every fact was verified, no matter what time and pains it needed' " (p. 127).

48 Mrs. H. Ward, *A Writer's Recollections*, Vol. I (New York and London: Harper, 1918), 140.

49 John Morley, "On Pattison's Memoirs," *Macmillan's Magazine*, LI (April 1885), 446-461; rptd. in John Morley, *Nineteenth Century Essays*, ed. Peter Stansky (Chicago and London: University of Chicago Press, 1970), p. 326. See also Morley's account of Pattison's essay on deism and the philosophical bent of his thought in Morley's *Recollections*, Vol. I (New York: Macmillan, 1917), 72.

50 See Dilke's "Memoir," *The Book of the Spiritual Life*, pp. 26-27.

51 *The Book of the Spiritual Life*, p. 85.

52 See Kingsbury Badger, "Mark Pattison and the Victorian Scholar," pp. 423-427.

53 [Lady Dilke], "*Imaginary Portraits*. by Walter Pater, M. A.," *Athenaeum*, no. 3113 (25 June 1887), 824-825.

54 See "Memoir," *The Book of the Spiritual Life*," p. 83.

55 See "Marius the Epicurean," *Atlantic Monthly*, LVI (August 1885), 273-277; see also *Pall Mall Gazette*, 18 March 1885, pp. 4-5; and Julia Wedgwood, "Fiction," *Contemporary Review*, XLVII (May 1885), 750-751, who faults the book for its attempt to translate nineteenth-century feeling into the age of Marcus Aurelius.

56 For Beerbohm's quote, see "Whistler's Writing," in *Yet Again* (London: Chapman and Hall, 1909); rptd. (New York: Knopf, 1928), p. 104. For the lines from Symonds' letter, see his letter to Henry Graham Dakyns, quoted in Monsman's *Walter Pater*, p. 63.

[57] See J. A. Symonds, "Art and Archaeology," *Academy*, IV (15 March 1873), 103-105.

[58] See *Essays Speculative and Suggestive* (London: Chapman and Hall, 1890); rptd. (New York: Scribners, 1894), pp. 358-361.

[59] Phyllis Grosskurth, *John Addington Symonds: A Biography* (London: Longmans, 1964), pp. 205-206. Grosskurth notes that Symonds, though constantly advocating how much he learned from the common folk, "was never very explicit what these lessons were beyond the fact that ... they were far more tolerant towards sexual deviation" (p. 206).

[60] *Essays Speculative and Suggestive*, pp. 273-274.

[61] *Ibid.*, p. 262.

[62] *Ibid.*, p. 437.

[63] *Ibid.*, p. 437.

CHAPTER II: WELL-INTENDED REVIEWERS

[1] Stephen Potter, *The Muse in Chains: A Study in Education* (London: Jonathan Cape, 1937); rptd. (Folcroft, Pa.: Folcroft Library Editions), p. 135.

[2] Sir Herbert Grierson, "Some Personal Memoirs," in *A Saintsbury Miscellany* (New York: Oxford University Press, 1947), p. 11.

[3] John Gross, *The Rise and Fall of the Man of Letters: A Study of the Idiosyncratic and the Humane in Modern Literature* (New York: Macmillan, 1969), p. 144. Gross suggests that we read Saintsbury to find out what Saintsbury has been reading; "one usually carries away from him a dazed impression of how much he knows about this and that, rather than anything particular which he has to say about the subject in hand" (p. 144).

[4] See his entry on "John Wilson" in *Encyclopaedia Brittannica*, Vol. XXIV (1900), 591-593.

[5] *The Rise and Fall of the Man of Letters*, p. 142.

[6] Potter, *The Muse in Chains*, p. 132; on Saintsbury's students, Potter notes that they now have high praise for Saintsbury: "to them he was a personality—even vigorous, anti-academic, half swashbuckling, almost Elizabethan, antipedant." As a lecturer, however, he was not good: "He spoke from skeleton notes only, from little cards, with rather indecipherable headings written across them. It is said that there was 'some terrible disorder in the talk, with loose ends, pick-ups, recoveries, allusive asides' " (pp. 131-132).

[7] See *A Saintsbury Miscellany*, pp. 217-218.

[8] The Herrick essay was originally published in 1892 as an introduction to an edition of Herrick's poetry published by G. Bell and Sons; the essay was reprinted in *A Saintsbury Miscellany*, pp. 112-123.

9 See "Modern English Prose," *Fortnightly Review*, XIX (February 1876), 243-259.

10 See *Collected Essays and Papers of George Saintsbury 1875-1920*, Vol. III (1923); rptd. (Freeport, N.Y.: Books for Libraries Press, 1969), p. 87.

11 See *A History of Nineteenth Century Literature (1780-1895)* (London and New York: Macmillan, 1896), pp. 398-401.

12 See "Walter H. Pater," in *English Prose Selections*, ed. by Henry Craik (London and New York: Macmillan, 1896), Vol. V, 747-750.

13 See *A History of English Prose Rhythm* (London: Macmillan, 1912), pp. 420-426.

14 See Webster, "A Biographical Memoir," in *A Saintsbury Miscellany*, p. 55; see also Saintsbury's *A History of English Prose Rhythm*, p. 421; Pater is supposed to have acknowledged, in response to Saintsbury's compliment that the paragraph is never sacrificed to the sentence in Pater's prose, that special care for the paragraph was "one of his principal objects." See also, *Letters of Walter Pater*, p. 171.

15 Herbert Read, "George Saintsbury," *Spectator*, CLI (22 December 1933), 938; rptd. in *A Coat of Many Colours: Occasional Essays* (London: Routledge and Sons, 1945), p. 199.

16 Wendell Harris, "The Critics," in *Victorian Prose: A Guide to Research*, ed. David DeLaura (New York: Modern Language Association, 1973), p. 455. Harris adds, "Saintsbury rejects any form of identification of art with morality or with 'a criticism of life.' The relationship of literature to other forms of thought and cultural expression is thus severed."

17 See Levine and Madden, "Introduction," *The Art of Victorian Prose*, ed. by Levine and Madden (New York: Oxford University Press, 1968), p. xi; "it was Pater . . . who first advanced the claim that the prose essay was *the* characteristic modern literary genre, and Pater's self-consciousness produced, within a short time, the overbalance suggested by Saintsbury's remark . . . that style was 'an arrangment of words with meaning subordinate.' It was against this kind of dilettantism that the reaction initiated by Eliot and other critics early in this century was directed" (p. xi); for an opinion on Saintsbury's failure to read Pater correctly, see Dorothy Richardson, "Saintsbury and Art for Art's Sake in England," *PMLA*, LIX (1944), 243-260.

18 The review was reprinted in Pater's *Essays from the 'Guardian'* (London: Macmillan, 1910), see especially p. 15. Pater writes, "in style, as in other things, it is well always to aim at the combination of as many excellences as possible. . . . there are still some who think that . . . the style is the man; justified . . . by the simple consideration of what he himself has to say, quite independently of any real or supposed connection with this or that literary age or school." But Pater calls on "the most versatile master of English," Cardinal Newman, to respond to the argument from style and with this directive he concludes his review: Newman observes " 'that the mere dealer in words cares little or nothing for the subject which he is embellish-

ing, but can paint and gild anything whatever to order; whereas the artist ... has his great or rich visions before him ...' " (pp. 15-16). The quote from Newman had to be intended as a mild rebuke to those, including Saintsbury, who would put style before subject matter.

[19] See "Saintsbury and Art for Art's Sake in England," *PMLA*, p. 255.

[20] See Malcolm Edwin, *Old Gods Falling* (New York: Macmillan, 1939), p. 306. Elwin notes that Mrs. Ward was "a painfully earnest woman. ... She wore blue stockings almost from babyhood, going early to the Ambleside school of Miss Anne Clough ... where she daily absorbed the atmosphere till lately breathed by Wordsworth, and at fourteen she would feel faint with gladness at the news of her father's reversion from Roman Catholicism and make notes in her diary on hearing 'a droll sermon on Convictional Sin'. ... she ever exuded the camphorated culture of the Banbury Road. At fourteen, she seemed seventeen ..." (p. 306).

[21] *A Writer's Recollections*, I, 160-161.

[22] *Ibid.*, I, 162.

[23] *Ibid.*, I, 163.

[24] See "*Marius the Epicurean*" in *Macmillan's Magazine*, LII (June 1885), 132-139; especially, 136-137.

[25] *Ibid.*, pp. 137-138.

[26] *Ibid.*, p. 138.

[27] *Ibid.*, p. 138.

[28] See *Letters of Walter Pater*, pp. 60-61. Pater writes, "To be really understood by a critic at once so accomplished and so generous as yourself, is a real reward for one's labours. When one has taken pains about a piece of work, it is certainly pleasant to have a criticism upon it which is itself so graceful and painstaking."

[29] *A Writer's Recollections*, I, 162-163.

[30] *Ibid.*, I, 163.

[31] See *Letters of Walter Pater*, pp. 60-61.

[32] "*Marius the Epicurean*," *Macmillan's Magazine*, p. 137; she notes that "its principal intellectual weakness ... is the further application of this Epicurean principle of an aesthetic loss and gain not only to morals, but to religion. ... Just as adhesion to the accepted moral order enriches and beautifies the experience of the individual, and so gives a greater savour and attractiveness to life, so acquiescence in the religious order ... opens for him opportunities of feeling and sensation which would otherwise be denied him."

[33] See *Letters of Walter Pater*, pp. 64-65.

[34] *A Writer's Recollections*, II, 40.

[35] "*Marius the Epicurean*," *Macmillan's Magazine*, p. 133.

[36] The review was reprinted as "Amiel's 'Journal Intime,' " in *Essays from the 'Guardian,'* pp. 17-37.

[37] The review was reprinted as "Robert Elsmere" in *Essays from the 'Guardian,'* pp. 53-70.

[38] See Monsman, *Walter Pater*, pp. 100-104. Monsman suggests that "because Marius attains to Christianity within the primitive church of the apostles and martyrs, not the church of the *Summa Theologiae*, it would be unhistorical to expect from him a theologically reasoned assent. Indeed, Pater deliberately sought that phase of Christianity in which the sources of religious assent had not yet become entangled in the dogma of the theologians" (p. 102).

[39] Julia Wedgwood called *Marius*, in direct contrast to Mrs. Ward's conclusion, a novel "too purely intellectual"—see "Fiction," *Contemporary Review*, XLVII (May 1885), 750-751; an anonymous reviewer for *Westminster Review* noted that as an examination of the merits of Christianity "tinctured with a sort of select aestheticism," the novel was "dreary"—see "Contemporary Literature. Belles Lettres," *Westminster Review*, LXIX (January 1886), 594-595; J. M. Gray in *Academy* cited Pater's extensive detailing in *Marius* of "the difficulties and weaknesses" of Epicureanism but offered no argument for the review as a testament of faith—see "Literature," *Academy*, XXVII (21 March 1885), 197-199; Alfred Goodwin in *Mind* concluded that the novel left the reader with an impression of "hopelessness in regard to systems, mixed with a remarkable religiosity and belief in the individual desire to believe"—see "Critical Notices: W. Pater, *Marius the Epicurean*," *Mind*, X (July 1885), 442-447; Edward Woodberry in *Nation* (NY) observed that he saw neither how the aesthetic morality worked in the book nor what good came of it—see "Ideal Aestheticism," *Nation* (NY), XLI (10 September 1885), 219-221.

[40] See "Two Roman Novels," *Edinburgh Review*, CLXV (January 1887), 248-267; "The Theology of Walter Pater," *British Weekly*, XXI (31 December 1896), 197-198; "*Gaston de Latour: an Unfinished Romance*," *Athenaeum*, no. 3599 (17 October 1896), 518-519; Vernon Lee, *Renaissance Fancies and Studies* (London: Smith, Elder, 1896), pp. 255-260; Stanley Addelshaw, "Walter Pater," *Gentleman's Magazine*, CCLXXXII (March 1897), 227-251.

[41] Benson, *Walter Pater*, p. 90.

[42] The letter to Vernon Lee is quoted in Benson, *Walter Pater*, pp. 89-90; see also *Letters of Walter Pater*, pp. 51-52.

[43] D. S. MacColl, "A Batch of Memories. XII—Walter Pater," *The Weekend Review*, December 12, 1931, pp. 759-760.

[44] See Janet Penrose Trevelyan, *The Life of Mrs. Humphry Ward* (New York: Dodd, Mead, 1923), p. 99; see also *Letters of Walter Pater*, p. 127.

[45] See Gosse's "Preface" to *Selected Essays*, first series (London: Heinemann, 1928).

[46] For an account of the Collins-Gosse conflict, see Stephen Potter, *The Muse in Chains*, pp. 189-192; John Gross, *The Rise and Fall of the Man of Letters*, pp. 159-161; and Malcolm Elwin, *Old Gods Falling*, pp. 202-204; Collins' original attack on Gosse's *From Shakespeare to Pope* appeared in *Quarterly Review*, CLXIII (October 1885), 289-329; for information on Collins' review of Gosse's *Short History of Modern English Literature*, see Elwin, p. 203.

[47] See, for example, James D. Woolf, *Sir Edmund Gosse* (New York: Twayne, 1972), pp. 49-58.

[48] Gross, *The Rise and Fall of the Man of Letters*, pp. 158-163.

[49] Elwin, *Old Gods Falling*, p. 205.

[50] "Walter Pater. A Portrait," *Critical Kit-Kats*, pp. 261-264.

[51] *Ibid.*, pp. 264-265.

[52] *Ibid.*, p. 260.

[53] *Ibid.*, pp. 267-268.

[54] See Evans, *Letters of Walter Pater*, p. xxxvi.

[55] See the essay on Whitman in *Critical Kit-Kats*, pp. 97, 111.

[56] See "Mr. Pater on Platonism," *New Review* (April 1893), p. 421.

[57] *Ibid.*, p. 426.

[58] *Ibid.*, p. 429.

[59] See *Life and Letters of Mandell Creighton ... By His Wife* (London: Longmans, Green, 1904).

[60] Henry James, *Letters*, Vol. I, ed. Percy Lubbock (New York: Scribner's, 1920), 221-222.

[61] See "The Present Position of English Criticism," *Time* (London), XIII (December 1885), 669-678; especially 674-675.

[62] Gosse, *Short History of Modern English Literature* (New York: Appleton, 1897); rptd. (1898), pp. 383-384.

[63] "Walter Pater. A Portrait," *Critical Kit-Kats*, p. 271.

CHAPTER III: JOHN MORLEY: THE POSITIVE TURN OF MIND

[1] Basil Willey, *More Nineteenth Century Studies: A Group of Honest Doubters* (New York: Columbia University Press, 1956); rptd. (New York: Harper and Row, 1966), p. 249. Morley deserves to be revalued by students and historians of Victorian literature and ideas. "In the 'history of ideas' (or in his own phrase, of 'opinion') his studies of Burke, De Maistre, Rousseau, Diderot and many others show him as an eminent pioneer, and his *On Compromise*, though it lacks the gracefulness of *Culture and Anarchy*, can be classed with it as a responsible critique on the times" (pp. 248-249).

[2] Edward Alexander, *John Morley* (New York: Twayne, 1972), p. 174.

[3] Willey, *More Nineteenth Century Studies*, p. 248. Willey writes that Morley, "was one of the most influential critics of his time, sharing the literary and intellectual dictatorship only, perhaps, with Leslie Stephen and Matthew Arnold.... And although questions on Morley are never found in university examinations on Victorian literary criticism, his essays on Macaulay, Carlyle, Byron, Browning and Wordsworth (to mention no more) are quite as worthy of inclusion in the canon as some of Arnold's" (pp. 248-249).

[4] See Mrs. Ward's *A Writer's Recollections*, II, 2f.

[5] Morley's review of Swinburne's *Poems and Ballads* appeared in *Saturday Review* for August 4, 1866; his review of Browning was reprinted in *Studies in Literature* (London: Macmillan, 1897), pp. 255-285.

[6] See Morley's *Critical Miscellanies*, Vol. I (London: Macmillan, 1898), 210.

[7] See Morley's *Recollections*, I, 97. Of his editorship and the goals of the journal, Morley writes, "our miscellany of writers and subjects was soon taken by prejudiced observers to disclose an almost sinister unity in spirit and complexion. This unity was in fact the spirit of liberalism in its most many-sided sense. Chilly welcome was extended to those promiscuous persons whom Treitschke found so terribly numerous at the present day—who will offer you now a remark on the Sistine Madonna, now an opinion on Bonapartism, now an observation on the steam-engine—'seldom anything absolutely stupid, but more seldom still anything shrewdly to the point.' Yet the genial can certainly not have been altogether banished from pages that were honoured with work from Arnold, Swinburne, Meredith, Gabriel Rossetti, Bagehot, Huxley, Pater, Lewes, Harrison, Dicey, Leslie Stephen, Pattison, Myers" (p. 86).

[8] See *Recollections*, I, 85-90; see also Edwin Mallard Everett, *The Party of Humanity* (Chapel Hill, N.C.: University of North Carolina Press, 1939), for a thorough account of the history of the *Fortnightly* from 1865 to 1874.

[9] See the account in F. W. Hirst, *Early Life and Letters of John Morley*, Vol. I (London: Macmillan, 1927), 288.

[10] Spender recounts the story in "John Morley" in *Fortnightly* (December 1938) ; see F. W. Knickerbocker's study of *Free Minds: John Morley and His Friends* (Cambridge, Mass.: Harvard University Press, 1943), p. 111.

[11] See Knickerbocker, p. 112; see also Morley's "Memorials of a Man of Letters" and his "Valedictory," written in October 1882 upon leaving the editorship of *Fortnightly*; both essays are reprinted in Morley, *Studies in Literature*, pp. 286-322; 323-347; and in Morley, *Nineteenth-Century Essays*, ed. Peter Stansky, pp. 261-280; 281-293.

[12] See Knickerbocker, *Free Minds: John Morley and His Friends*, p. 112.

[13] *Recollections*, I, 104-105.

[14] *Recollections,* I, 68-69; "Some two University generations before my own, Oxford had sent to London a remarkable group of disciples of Comte. This group became known to me through Lewes and George Eliot, who were both of them ... adherents of Comtist doctrines" (p. 68).

[15] *Recollections,* I, 71; "Still, resolute equity and diligent breadth of outlook in assigning its place to an opinion was one aspect of the rise of what we easily sum up in talking of the historic method, and the triumph of the principle of relativity in historic judgment. The great intellectual conversion of this era, as Renan not any too widely put it, transformed the science of language into the history of languages; transformed the science of literature and philosophies into their histories; the science of the human mind into its history, not merely an analysis of the wheel-work and propelling forces of the individual soul. In other words, the marked progress of criticism and interpretation of life has been the substitution of *becoming* for *being,* the relative for the absolute, dynamic movement for dogmatic immobility" (pp. 71-72).

[16] Gerald Monsman, *Walter Pater,* p. 28; Monsman plays down the *Fortnightly* influence in favor of the influence of the "predominantly Positivist philosophy of the *Westminster Review*" in which Pater's earliest studies were published; he notes that the empirical-scientific spirit of those studies owes much to Pater's familiarity with the works of Mill, Lewes, and Sir William Hamilton on Comte, as well as Huxley, Spencer, Tyndall, St. G. Mivart, W. K. Clifford, and other scientific writers of the time (p. 28).

[17] "Leonardo da Vinci," *The Renaissance* (1910), pp. 109-110, 111, 125-126, 128-129.

[18] "Mr. Pater's Essays," *Fortnightly Review,* XIII (April 1873); rptd. in Morley, *Nineteenth-Century Essays,* ed. Peter Stansky, p. 233.

[19] Alexander, *John Morley,* pp. 172-173.

[20] Alexander, *John Morley,* p. 174; Alexander observes that "Morley did not ... persuade himself that Pater was really a Positivist; but he saw that Pater, like himself, recognized the changed intellectual circumstances within which the artist now had to function" (p. 174).

[21] In *Recollections,* I, 306, Morley writes of having thrown the two books out of the window with the hope that the French peasantry would be lucky enough never to learn to read. He does not identify the books; the date was January 16, 1892. In response to the story, Lytton Strachey, Nemesis for all things Victorian, observed that only a Victorian, having made his reputation by writing the lives of French intellectuals, would have thrown two French novels in horror out of the window. Even the Victorian atheists were finally religious, Strachey claims. See Willey, *More Nineteenth Century Studies,* p. 248.

[22] See *Early Life and Letters of John Morley,* I, 207.

[23] "A Few Words on French Models," *Studies in Literature,* p. 161.

[24] See "A Few Words on French Models," *Studies in Literature,* p. 160;

"whether the present writer does or does not deserve all the compliments that history has paid to Saint-Just, is a very slight and trivial question, with which the public will naturally not much concern itself.... Only on the principle that who drives fat oxen must himself be fat, can it be held that who writes on Danton must be himself in all circumstances a Dantonist" (pp. 160-161).

[25] The reference to Adele's French mother appears in chapter 15. In the same chapter, Rochester notes that he had rescued Adele, "the poor thing," from "the slime and mud of Paris, and transplanted [her] here, to grow up clean in the wholesome soil of an English country garden."

[26] The letter of 4 November 1882 was printed in *William Sharp: A Memoir*, by Elizabeth A. Sharp (New York: Duffield, 1910), p. 68; rptd. in *Letters of Walter Pater*, pp. 43-45.

[27] See especially his essays on "Vézelay" and "Notre-Dame d'Amiens" in *Miscellaneous Studies* (London: Macmillan, 1910).

[28] See *The Renaissance*, pp. xxii-xxiii.

[29] See Knickerbocker, p. 191, for the date of the original publication; the essay is reprinted in *Studies in Literature*, pp. 229-254.

[30] See "Victor Hugo's 'Ninety-Three,' " *Studies in Literature*, pp. 234-236.

[31] *Ibid.*, pp. 241-242, 247.

[32] "The Poetry of Michelangelo," *The Renaissance*, p. 74.

[33] "Two Early French Stories," *The Renaissance*, pp. 24-25.

[34] Morley, *Recollections*, I, 73-74.

[35] "The Poetry of Michelangelo," *The Renaissance*, p. 97.

[36] "Conclusion," *The Renaissance*, pp. 238-239.

[37] See Warren Staebler, *The Liberal Mind of John Morley* (Princeton: Princeton University Press, 1943), p. 41. Staebler writes that "Comte's scheme for including in Humanity's Pantheon all those who had contributed notably to the march of civilization" found favor with Morley, and "it assisted the growth of his historical broadmindedness" as well as accounting for his interest in men so mutually antagonistic (p. 41).

[38] "Mr. Pater's Essays," in *Nineteenth-Century Essays*, ed. Peter Stansky, p. 236.

[39] *Early Life and Letters of John Morley*, I, 240.

[40] "Mr. Pater's Essays," in *Nineteenth-Century Essays*, ed. Peter Stansky, p. 235.

[41] *Ibid.*, pp. 235-236.

[42] The criticism by "Z" appeared in the *Examiner*, no. 3402 (12 April 1873), pp. 381-382; Morley's reply appeared a week later in no. 3403 (19 April 1873), p. 410.

[43] See "Byron," *Critical Miscellanies*, I, 213-215; Morley writes that "Byron ... is never moved by the strength of his passion or the depth of his contemplation quite away from the round earth and the civil animal who dwells upon it. Even his misanthropy is only an inverted form of social solicitude. His practical zeal for good and noble causes might teach us this. He never grudged either money or time or personal peril for the cause of Italian freedom, and his life was the measure and the cost of his interest in the liberty of Greece.... It was this which made Byron a social force, a far greater force than Shelley either has been or can be. Men read in each page that he was one of like passions with themselves; that he had their own feet of clay, if he had other members of brass and gold and fine silver which they had none of; and that vehement sensibility ... had not obliterated, but had rather quickened, the sense of the highest kind of man of the world, which did not decay but waxed stronger in him with years" (pp. 215-216).

[44] "Mr. Pater's Essays," in *Nineteenth-Century Essays*, ed. Peter Stansky, p. 228.

[45] *Ibid.*, p. 229.

[46] See *On Compromise* (London: Macmillan, 1903), pp. 71-72.

[47] "Mr. Pater's Essays," in *Nineteenth-Century Essays*, ed. Peter Stansky, p. 231.

[48] *Ibid.*, p. 231.

[49] *Ibid.*, p. 236.

[50] See "On the Study of Literature" in *Studies in Literature*, pp. 193-194; the address was delivered on 26 February 1887 at the Mansion House.

[51] Alexander, in *John Morley*, offers the soundest theory for Morley's neglect in the twentieth century. He observes that the reasons are both literary and political. "Like many Victorians, he appears to modern readers to have lived too long. The image of Morley as a superannuated relic of the nineteenth century who tried to keep the twentieth century from being born can be confirmed by such evidence as his notorious reader's report, in 1900, to Macmillan's on the work of a young Irish poet: 'I would not read a page of it again for worlds, and I care not how many good judges swear that 'Yeats ought to have his chance! ... There is no saying in these rather demented days what an industrious band of admirers may not succeed in foisting into an ephemeral popularity.'" John Gross comments that although Morley is not talking about Yeats at his best in this report, it is " 'by comparison with anything that Morley ever wrote, enough to burn a hole in the page.' " By the twentieth century, Alexander concludes, the avant-garde editor of the *Fortnightly* had come to see "the progeny of Walter Pater, whom he had himself promoted, as the characteristic offspring of "these rather demented days." Owing to Morley's response to the "demented days" there has developed in the twentieth century indifference or "downright hostility" to him. "Modern social critics have assumed Morley to be an easy and inviting target." He is "condescendingly called 'a

nineteenth-century liberal' " who is supposed to have betrayed his own liberal principles. But Morley's only weakness, Alexander suggests, is that "he did not always reach the perfection of his own ideal" (pp. 186-187).

[52] "A Few Words on French Models," *Studies in Literature*, p. 163.

[53] "Mr. Pater's Essays," in *Nineteenth-Century Essays*, ed. Peter Stansky, p. 215.

[54] Basil Willey, *More Nineteenth Century Studies*, p. 291.

[55] See *Early Life and Letters of John Morley*, I, 240; see also *Letters of Walter Pater*, pp. 21-22.

committee party itself." [text illegible]

the only source quoted [text illegible]

A few [text illegible]

Mr. Paine's essay [text illegible]

"Basil Williams, *Whitefoord Papers*, pp. [illegible]

See *Life and Letters of John Kearsey Philips*; see also *Gibbs of ... Papers*, pp. 47-52.